ACKNOWLEDGEMENTS

Many people have helped this book into being. I should particularly like to thank my clients over the years, fellow psychologists Tony Black, Bernard Kat and Chris Leach, editor Joyce Collins, and my husband, Kevin McConway.

Grateful thanks are also due to: Sylvia Bell, Georgina Cuthbertson, John Elliott, Chris Gillespie, Gail Hawks, Alanah Houston, David Jones, Cheryl Mitchel, Elizabeth Quickstrom, Mo Shapiro, Dorothy Welchman and Dave Waddilove.

CONTENTS

Chapter 1

'It must be psychological' or 'It's your nerves' are common enough remarks. But when it comes to psychological problems, what are the common ones, and how can people be helped?

Who is this book for?

This book is for you if you are an adult and you feel you have a psychological problem or have been told you have one. It may also be useful for other family members and friends. If you are consistently unhappy, or if there are problems which you think you should be able to cope with but can't, then perhaps some kind of psychological treatment is for you. This book won't do the treatment for you, but it will give you some idea of what to expect from your therapist. (This book will also be useful for health and social service professionals or people in the voluntary sector who want an introduction to current psychological outpatient treatments.) It does not cover the special problems of children or the more severe adult psychiatric problems such as manic depression or schizophrenia. Nor does it cover drug or medical treatments (such as electro-convulsive therapy) or inpatient treatments.

The very idea of having a 'mental' problem or going for some sort of psychological treatment makes some people worry that they are going mad or out of their mind. They may also worry that having to ask for help means they are weak or inferior, stupid or bad. These myths, added to the fear of the unknown and not understanding the problem, can only add to the person's distress. The result is a loss of confidence and self-esteem. But reading the case histories of people with common psychological problems will show you quite clearly that these worries are unfounded. So, if you think you have a psychological problem, don't suffer alone. If you need help, ask for it. (Some of the main sources of help are discussed in Chapter 5.)

If you have a problem you are likely to have several questions:

☐ HOW can someone help me?

☐ WHAT kind of help can I get?

☐ HOW can I find help?

☐ WHO can help?

The aim of this book is to answer these questions.

This is not a self-help manual

This book is not a self-help manual. It does not set out to provide enough information for you to tackle your problems entirely on your own. Instead it describes psychological therapies which are used by professionals working with the person who has the problem. These treatments have been well-tried and tested.

The size of the problem

If you have a psychological problem, you probably feel very much alone. But problems of anxiety, depression, difficulty in sleeping, irritability, worrying thoughts, obsessions, compulsions and phobias are reasonably common. Something like a third of the people visiting their doctor each day have psychological problems of some sort. And many of these problems get better without any treatment. But even when people have a clear physical illness or disorder they can be affected psychologically as well. Examples of this are given later, in Chapter 3.

A few people don't visit their doctor at all to discuss their psychological problems. Of those who do go to the doctor, some go back time after time with minor physical problems before finally getting round to discussing the main thing that is worrying them. Or they may be treated for physical ailments before the doctor recognizes that the physical symptoms are linked with psychological difficulties. A psychological problem may not be their reason for visiting the doctor, or it may be one of several problems they want to discuss.

Only a very few people are referred on to see a psychiatrist. Most of these will be treated as outpatients and will not have to stay in hospital. One British review looked at what would happen to the 250 people with psychological problems out of every 1000 in the general population in any one year. Of these 250 people, 230 will visit their GP. The GP will recognize the problem in 140 of them. Seventeen will go on for specialist psychiatric treatment but only six will have treatment in a psychiatric hospital or unit.

What is this book about?

By looking at individual case histories, this book describes some of the common psychological problems among adults and the psychological treatments used for them. Most of these problems could be described as 'neuroses'.

It is not about the major mental illnesses known as 'psychoses'. Someone who is suffering from a psychotic illness tends to lose contact with reality. They experience sensations and thoughts unrelated to the outside world as we know it. So, for example, they may think that someone is sending them special messages through the television, which no one else can understand. Usually sufferers from psychoses do not think there is anything wrong with them, but other people see the changes and odd behaviour. People with psychotic illnesses are usually best helped by a psychiatrist, most often with drugs, and sometimes with the involvement of a multi-disciplinary team of different mental health professionals.

No book as short as this can claim to be comprehensive. This book concentrates on one general approach to therapy – a cognitive-behavioural one – in the case histories in Chapter 3. (This and other major approaches to therapy are briefly outlined in Chapter 4.)

This book helps you to look at how you can get the most out of psychological treatment yourself, and it looks at the professionals who might offer such treatments. Finally, it looks at the profession of psychology itself, and answers some of the questions people ask about clinical psychologists in particular. Further reading is suggested at the end of each section, where appropriate, and at the end of the book. Useful addresses for getting books by post are also given at the end.

2. Waiting For An Appointment

▽ *What exactly is the problem?*
▽ *What do you want to get out of treatment?*
▽ *The pros and cons of treatment for you.*
▽ *Working together on the problem.*
▽ *Homework is half the battle.*

This chapter looks at some of the things you might like to consider if you are thinking of getting help for a psychological problem, or while you are on the waiting list for psychological treatment. It also discusses some general issues in psychological treatments.

WHAT EXACTLY IS THE PROBLEM?

If you are wanting some sort of help, then naturally you feel you have a problem. At first, problems, although worrying, are very often quite unclear. For example, Brendan said: 'My partner and I do not seem to be sexually compatible'. Fiona's worry was: 'I can't talk to people. I just feel terrible'. Clearer descriptions of these individuals' problems could be: 'We have intercourse once a month and neither of us enjoys it much even though we both have an orgasm. I am frightened that we are drifting apart, and my partner may start looking elsewhere'. And: 'I feel very frightened when I have to talk to someone I don't know very well, so I try to avoid doing so whenever I can. It means they won't even consider me for promotion at work'.

Both of these now give a somewhat clearer picture of both the current problem, and what the person fears will happen if the problem continues. In some cases, what at first appears to be the problem is actually a faulty solution to an earlier, more basic problem.

Part of the job of the therapist is to help you to clarify the problem, as then you can agree exactly what it is you want to work together on changing. To some extent, how therapists define a problem depends on the theory they use to understand psychology, and on the treatment methods they use. For more on this see Chapter 4 on some different approaches to therapy.

It will be helpful both to you and your therapist if you can start with a reasonably clear idea of what the problem is. In some cases this is quite straightforward. In others it takes much more time and skill, particularly if the problem has been going on for some time, or if there are a number of different problems.

One way of beginning to understand a problem is to keep a record of when it occurs. On page 7 is part of a record form which was used by someone who, through anxiety, could not write in front of other people. He was working to overcome the problem as he was getting married in four months' time, and wanted to sign the Register with his close relatives around him.

WHAT DO YOU WANT TO GET OUT OF TREATMENT?

Before you see a therapist, it is worth asking yourself what you want to get out of the treatment. What do you want to be doing differently by the end of treatment? Do you want to feel different? If you want another person to change (who isn't involved in treatment), you are probably setting unrealistic goals. Should anyone else be involved apart from you and the therapist? If so, who?

Deciding what you want out of treatment, or setting treatment goals, is something you will discuss with your therapist. However, before you meet you can give this subject some thought yourself. Questions you can ask yourself are:

? *How will I know when I have got what I want out of treatment?*

? *What will I be doing that is different from now, if the treatment is successful?*

? *Can I break down my final goal into several smaller goals?*

Date	Circumstances	How I felt	What I did
8 April	In bank writing cheque	Shaky. Sure people stared.	Pretended to read leaflets until other customers left.
10 April	In lecture taking notes.	Uptight	Sat at the back so no one could see me.
13 April	Asked to write my address.	Shaky. Trapped.	Said I didn't have a pen but I would post it.

Remember Fiona who felt frightened talking to strangers? Here is part of her list of goals. At the bottom of the list is the main thing she is aiming to do. The items before that are her smaller subgoals. By taking each of these in turn, it makes it more likely that she will reach her main goal. It may be that she won't actually reach the end of her list (or hierarchy) during treatment. However, it helped her to define a direction to work in.

① Practice relaxation every day.

② Say 'Hello' to the receptionist on my way to the office each morning.

③ Go to the library and ask where books on France are kept.

④ Go into three large shops and ask if they stock a particular item.

⑤ Ask for ten pence pieces in my change at the newsagents.

/

/

/

/

⑩ Join an evening class to learn to play Bridge.

Imagine the main goal as something you want to reach at the top of a staircase. On each step is a subgoal, with the one that seems easiest to reach on the bottom step, the one that seems next easiest to reach on the second step, and so on. Each step is important: it's easiest to reach the top if you take each step steadily, rather than jumping over several at a time.

Working out your goals

→ To work out your own goal list, get a large piece of paper and a pen.

→ At the bottom of the page write down what you would ideally like to do if you had solved the problem. That is your final goal.

→ Then write what you can cope with now at the top of the page. Write '1' next to this.

→ Then write down all the other things you could do by way of overcoming the problem and reaching your final goal.

→ When you have written as many things as you can think of, you can put the steps in order. Write a '2' by the item which is next easiest after step '1'. Then write a '3' by the next easiest item and so on until you have been through all the items.

→ Then rewrite your list in order of difficulty.

PROS AND CONS OF TREATMENT FOR YOU

You may have mixed feelings about asking for help with a problem which is all or part psychological; many people do. So it's worth looking at the pros and cons of going for treatment. If you feel that, on the whole, the pros outweight the cons, you will be motivated to complete treatment. But if not, either you won't feel enthusiastic about treatment, or your practical difficulties will hinder you. Or maybe it is because you are depressed at the moment and don't see any point in anything. It might help to discuss your ideas of the pros and cons of treatment with someone else, who can point out anything you have missed, or who might be able to offer a different point of view.

Work out the pros and cons for yourself. Ask yourself the following questions and write down your answers in the appropriate column opposite.

Practical:

1. Can I get to the appointments? (E.g. Bus times? Use car?)

2. Can I arrange the time to go to the appointments? (E.g. Arrange time off work? Baby sitters?)

Personal:

3. How will I benefit if I overcome my problems?

4. What benefits, if any, do I gain from having this problem? So, what am I going to lose by solving the problem?

5. If this problem is solved, will people expect more from me than I can cope with?

6. If I change, how is it going to affect the people who are close to me? Will it put pressure on family, friends, or on me?

Therapy:

7. Do I particularly want to see a male or a female therapist, if given a choice?

8. Have I got strong feelings about the kind of therapy I want, if given a choice? (See Chapter 4.)

There may be other pros and cons that you would consider in your own case.

Pro	Con

Here is Fiona's list of pros and cons in response to these questions.

Pro	Con
Question 1 — It's easy to borrow the car if I have 2 days notice. The clinic is on our bus route anyway.	
Question 2	I don't want anyone at work to know I'm going, so I'll use flexitime to get the time off.
Question 3 — I'll be more independent. I won't have to wait for Bill to do the talking at parties, etc. I won't feel exhausted & suffer the terrible feelings when I'm anxious. I'd be more likely to get promotion, and more money.	
Questions 4/5/6	Bill is very protective of me and asks if I feel O.K. If I find it easier to talk to people, Bill will expect me to see more of his family, and deal with tradespeople etc. (I'm worried about the prospect of seeing more of my in-laws.) If I get promotion I may not be able to cope with the extra responsibility.
Questions 7/8	

No strong feelings.

She had never considered the ideas in questions 4, 5 and 6 before, and was surprised that she did gain some kind of benefit from having a fear of talking to people. She had thought that everything would be fine if she found it easier to talk to people, but when she thought about it a bit more she realised that overcoming the initial problem might open up new ones. These are shown in her answers to 4, 5 and 6. Despite this, she still wanted to go ahead with therapy, as the advantages for her in overcoming her fear were greater than the disadvantages. And if she tackled the fear first, she could tackle any other problems that might come up later.

WORKING TOGETHER ON THE PROBLEM

You will have gathered already that a person who is receiving psychological help is not passive. The way to get anything out of treatment is to work together with the therapist. And sometimes it is helpful to involve your spouse or a close friend also. Working *with* the therapist means taking an active part in the sessions, rather than sitting back and waiting for something to be done 'to' you. It means spending some time at the beginning making clear exactly what you and the therapist are both going to contribute to the therapy. This is called a *THERAPY CONTRACT*. It may only be spoken, or may be written down. The purpose of a contract is to clarify what your aims are, and how you are going to go about reaching them. It is not legally binding. It also usually means doing some kind of homework on the problem between sessions.

HOMEWORK IS HALF THE BATTLE

The word homework conjures up pictures of evenings after school, reading and writing. Most homework for psychological problems is nothing like that. Your therapist might suggest something for you to read; usually to back up what you have discussed and done in the session. But more often, homework involves practising what you did with the therapist in the session, or carrying out something you both discussed.

Homework can be done alone, or it might involve a relative or friend as a 'cotherapist'. Usually a cotherapist like this will have been to the therapy sessions with you. One cotherapist was the sister of

Rose who had a phobia of shops. They lived near each other, and arranged to go to a local shop together, Rose went in the shop while her sister waited outside.

You are also likely to have other practical work to do. A wide range of things are possible here. For example, Fiona might do items 2 and 4 on her list of goals three times each for one homework. One psychologist describes the homework tasks or assignments that he suggests as 'living to a purpose'. The purpose is to reduce the main problem. So someone who has suffered anxiety in queues might go shopping as homework. The point is not just to buy things, but to have practice at keeping calm and coping with being in queues. When you do homework, it is usually a good idea to keep a written record of what you did.

3. Some Common Problems And Their Treatment

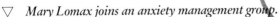

▽ *Mary Lomax joins an anxiety management group.*
▽ *John Sidman: cat phobic.*
▽ *Robert Smith: severely overweight.*
▽ *Shelley Pope: bulimia nervosa.*
▽ *Carol and Phil Stewart: overcoming sexual difficulties.*

This chapter gives examples of people with a range of problems and an outline of the treatments they received. A variety of professionals were involved as therapists, but all the treatments described in this chapter are used by clinical psychologists. For every person whose problem is described, a number of different treatments are available. The examples have been chosen to illustrate common problems that might be referred by a GP for outpatient treatment. They are based on the stories of real people but with details changed so that they cannot be identified.

The words 'treatment' or 'therapy' are usually used to describe the kind of help given. These words may give the impression that the person wanting help is passive, while a professional does something to them or for them, like when you are given an injection as a treatment. Not so: with psychological treatments or therapies the client is usually very active, and the work is done in partnership with the therapist. Sometimes treatment is carried out in groups of people with similar problems, as it was for Mary Lomax and Robert Smith in this chapter. No one can live your life for you or make decisions for you. But therapy can help you understand and decide, or look at and try new ways of thinking and behaving. In some cases the end of therapy is not the end of the story about that particular problem for the individual concerned. It might be the start of a new journey for the person involved, who now has new ways of thinking and solving problems for themselves.

The treatments may sound very simple and easy when you read about them, but most of them involved a lot of hard work and sometimes soul-searching for the person involved. Progress is not always steady. People do not always get on with their therapist, or they may take a while to get to like or trust them. This chapter looks at some of the more common psychological problems, as well as three cases in which psychological problems seem to follow from medical disorders. It does not cover all the problems treated by clinical psychologists and others, or all the treatments available.

ANXIETY-RELATED PROBLEMS

☐ *'I felt as if my heart was about to burst out of my chest it was beating so hard.'*

☐ *'I was so worried, I just couldn't think straight.'*

☐ *'I don't go to that supermarket now because I'm afraid that I'll get the awful feeling that I might pass out again.'*

☐ *'I felt as if I was watching it happen to someone else, as if I wasn't real.'*

These quotes are from people who sought professional help for their anxiety, but perhaps the first two comments might have been made by any one of us at a time of particular stress.

Anxiety can be helpful

Anxiety is something that everyone has experienced to some extent, and it can actually be helpful. If you see a fierce dog, the fight or flight reaction of your body can give you extra energy when you need it, so that you can run away fast. And the feeling that what is happening is not real or not happening to you can help protect you and help you to cope in dangerous situations. By becoming detached, it is as if your feelings switch off so you are less frightened. That allows you to keep thinking, so you can cope better with the danger. But if you get the feeling of being unreal at other times, when there is no apparent danger, or the sense that what is happening to you is actually happening to someone else, it is a symptom of anxiety and can be treated.

In the example just given, anxiety is a reaction to a real event, meeting a fierce dog. In other cases you can experience anxiety before actual events, in anticipation of them, like before a driving test or exam. If you get moderately anxious before an exam you are more likely to do your revision and then be alert and concentrate well on the exam itself. If, on the other hand, you are over-anxious, you will probably do badly. You feel dreadful, and your revision and performance in the exam itself go to pot.

Anxiety can become a problem

Anxiety becomes a problem if it interferes with what you want to do, or if it lasts long after the real danger (such as the fierce dog) has gone. It is also a problem if it happens when there is no real outside danger or if a person is afraid of a forthcoming event which is not in itself dangerous. It can become fear of fear itself, rather than fear of an actual event. For example, a woman who has suffered a panic attack in a supermarket might feel afraid of returning there in case she panics again. Fear itself then becomes a habit, related to thoughts and not to immediate situations. Anxiety is mainly a problem if you feel you can't cope with it on your own.

When anxiety is a problem needing treatment

A significant number of people visiting their GP are suffering from anxiety to some degree. Many of them complain of their physical symptoms, such as a pounding heart, the feeling of a knot in the stomach, sweating, tension or dizziness. Some of these symptoms might be due to overbreathing or hyperventilation. So when you try to control the feelings of panic by breathing deeply you only make yourself feel more dizzy. You need to learn regular, relaxed and shallow breathing.

Some people go to the doctor concerned with feeling that something dreadful is about to happen, but they don't know what, or that they are not able to get rid of worrying thoughts. Perhaps they notice that their memory or attention is not as good as it used to be. And some approach their doctor because of a change in behaviour. Perhaps they are avoiding travelling on buses, or meeting people, or they might be spending half an hour every morning checking that the lights are switched off before going to work.

In this section we look at two cases of people with anxiety-related problems and the treatments they received. One person, Mary Lomax, felt much of the time as if something awful was about to happen. She found an anxiety management group helped her. John Sidman only experienced severe anxiety when he came across cats, for which he had a phobia. He benefited from a desensitization programme in which he gradually learned to approach cats one step at a time.

The treatments described were appropriate for Mary and John as individuals, and for their particular problems. Mary could have had individual treatment, but she would not then have been able to learn from other group members, or share experiences with them. People like Mary and John are also treated using hypnosis or psychotherapy. Or they can read books for more information, and for self-help approaches. (A list of books and cassette tapes is given on pages 23-24.)

Mary Lomax JOINS AN ANXIETY MANAGEMENT GROUP

Mary went to her doctor for a physical check-up, as she had been feeling sick and dizzy. She always felt exhausted. And she felt that she could no longer cope with talking in front of groups of people, which was something she had done successfully for years. She had lost confidence, and usually had a terrible feeling that something awful was about to happen. She felt on tenter-hooks all the time.

Asking the doctor for help

Mary is 33 years old, unmarried, outgoing and a trained teacher. She works for a large computer company, running courses for new staff when they first join the company, and also refresher courses. She had never before had any sort of nervous trouble, and the problems she described to her doctor had only been going on for two months. She had had a lot of changes recently: she had moved house, been working hard on a new course which meant taking work home, and her best friend had moved away from the area.

After getting a picture of how the problem started, and how it affected Mary from day to day, her doctor explained that she was suffering from anxiety, and recommended that she see a psychologist who could help her learn practical ways of coping. The doctor said that minor tranquillizers might be useful in the short term, but they both agreed that a psychological approach, anxiety management, would be more useful in the long term.

Referral to a psychologist

Mary met the psychologist in his office in the District General Hospital. Their first meeting lasted about 50 minutes. The aim was to get a clear idea of her difficulties, and her own ideas about the kind of help she wanted. They would then be able to go on to make a plan of action for treatment. With the psychologist's careful listening and questioning, they arrived at an understanding of just what the problem was. He asked her questions about exactly how she felt and in what circumstances she felt anxious. They discussed the thoughts she had when she was feeling anxious. Mary also described the way her life was being affected, and what she now avoided doing as a result of these difficulties. The psychologist asked Mary what made it better, and what made it worse. He asked about the start of the problem, and the circumstances surrounding the onset of Mary's difficulties began to make sense to her.

Understanding the problem

The problems started when she had a panic attack during a teaching session. She was just recovering from 'flu, and had to present a session to a large group of people, including the company bigwigs. She had been worrying about it while she was still in bed with 'flu, as she had not had enough time to prepare. She had been in a rush that morning, missed breakfast, felt frustrated when she was held up by roadworks on the way to the office, and had two cups of coffee when she arrived. As she stood up to talk, she felt sick and very dizzy, as if she was about to pass out. Her mind went blank, and she just wanted to escape from what seemed like a huge sea of unsympathetic faces all staring at her. She made an excuse to look through her papers, recovered a little, and then managed to continue with the talk. However, she had a very strange feeling of being far away, as if it was all unreal, and she noticed she was sweating a great deal. She then cancelled the next teaching she had planned to do, saying that she needed longer to prepare the notes for it. She felt very uncomfortable going into the canteen, and began to eat sandwiches in her office instead. Also, when she went to the theatre or cinema she felt slightly sick and dizzy, but she did not let it put her off going to those places; and she found that after a while the feeling would pass.

Joining a group

The psychologist suggested to Mary that she join an anxiety management group, the aim of which was to teach people skills for coping with anxiety. The group would meet for one and a half hours each week for six weeks. It would be a 'closed' group, in that once it had started, the same people would remain throughout the course: you would not get new people joining half way through as happens in 'open' groups. He explained that they would cover a different topic each week, so it was best to attend every meeting, otherwise you would miss something. He then gave her a leaflet which gave an introduction to the course, and answered her questions.

Mary was keen to join the group, but felt very anxious waiting for the first meeting in two weeks' time. When she arrived she soon discovered that the eight other group members felt the same way and the ice was soon broken. It was quite informal and there was lots of opportunity for discussion, but no pressure to talk if you didn't want to. The psychologist emphasized confidentiality and everyone agreed not to talk about each other outside the group. Group members all filled in questionnaires describing their own experiences. The same questionnaires would be used again in six weeks' time, to see if there had been a change in symptoms.

Setting goals

In the first meeting the psychologist explained how you can understand and learn to cope with anxiety in terms of your feelings, your thoughts, and what you do. Each person set their own goals concerning what they wanted to do differently at the end of the course. Then they broke down each goal into a series of smaller steps, so that the first step was one they felt they could manage without much difficulty, and it would not be too big a jump from one step to the next. Mary's goals were to have lunch in the canteen at work four times a week, teach one class of ten students each week, and practise relaxation every day. Each week there was some homework to do which was an important part of the course – some sort of practical activity to keep a record of and discuss in the next meeting. Homework for the first week was just to keep a record of when you experienced anxiety. In later weeks Mary learned a method of relaxation which she continued to practise daily. With practice she was able to relax herself as soon as she noticed she was beginning to become tense or anxious. She also learned to recognize and then cope with her worrying thoughts. She began to set herself realistic goals so that she could tackle, step by step, the things she had been avoiding, and she learned how to reward herself for working towards her goals. All these things are skills that get better with regular practice.

For three members of the group, coming off minor tranquillizers was one of their goals. After discussion with the psychologist, they each wrote out a plan for gradually cutting down their tablets. For some this involved seeing their doctor to obtain lower dosage tablets or tablets which it would be easier to cut down. Each week they reported back on how they had coped and revised their goals if necessary. Some continued reducing their tablets after the group had finished meeting weekly.

At the end of the six weeks Mary had achieved all her goals, although she was still only going into the canteen when it was very quiet. She set herself further goals of eating there during the busy period between 12.30pm and 1pm four times a week, and teaching classes of 20 students, once a week. The questionnaires she had filled in showed a reduction in the number and severity of her symptoms, and Mary herself felt more confident knowing that she had developed skills to help her cope if she felt extremely anxious again. She was given the opportunity of continuing to attend monthly meetings of the anxiety management group if she wished to.

❖   ❖   ❖

John Sidman: CAT PHOBIC

John, 23, a teacher in a first school, was referred to the clinical psychologist at his local psychiatric day hospital for help with his phobia of cats. He had just started his first job, and was particularly keen to overcome his problem as the children were sometimes allowed to bring in their new pets. His main bugbear was that he wanted to ask out a young woman whom he knew to be a cat-lover, but did not dare to in case he looked foolish in front of her. He had no other significant difficulties. He felt confident about his job, his social life was enjoyable, and his childhood and educational history were all normal. However, he had been afraid of cats since about the age of five when his grandmother's cat had scratched him badly. His mother and grandmother made a great fuss of him at the time, and the cat was always shut away when he visited after that. His mother asked friends and relatives to keep cats away from John, saying that he didn't like them. Unwittingly, his well-meaning mother had prevented John from overcoming his fear.

Recently his phobia of cats had begun to affect him more and more. Whenever he was near a cat he would notice that he sweated profusely and had a feeling of sheer dread, although he told himself not to be silly. He said to himself things like: 'Look at those mean eyes. Horrible creature. It's out to get me. It'll spring any minute now.' No wonder he felt he had to keep his eyes on them all the time, and felt tense. He found slow-moving cats easier to cope with than fast-moving ones, and single cats easier than groups of cats. Worst of all was to be stuck in a confined space with the cat. He walked the long way to work in order to avoid an alley where two cats were often found. And had declined some invitations to colleagues' houses, as he knew they owned cats.

Breaking down the problem

With the psychologist, John wrote out a long list of situations involving cats which he wanted to learn to cope with:

☐ *Sit comfortably in an armchair in the lounge, while Harry sits in the armchair opposite, stroking a calm cat. Talk for 10 minutes.*

☐ Halfway down the list was:

Sit stroking a calm cat for ten minutes, talking to Harry.

☐ At the end of the list was:

Go to visit a colleague who has three cats and three kittens. Stroke all the cats for a total of ten minutes (minimum), and play with the kittens (ten minutes minimum).

They also made a list of John's thoughts when he worried about cats or actually encountered them. Most of these thoughts were negative, like the example given. Together, they worked out more useful responses, such as:

☐ *'What is it that is interesting about this individual cat?'*

The actual treatment involved exposing John to cats in real life. This was carried out by Harry, a psychiatric nurse, and supervised by the psychologist. In between weekly treatment sessions of about an hour, John would try to repeat what he had done in the session at home with the help of a friend. After eight treatment sessions, John could sit and stroke a cat for 20 minutes. He had visited the house of one of his pupils where there were two cats, and not felt anxious. He even surprised himself by saying, 'What a lovely looking cat!'

John was discharged from treatment after eight sessions. Although he had not got to the bottom of his list, he no longer avoided places where cats might be, nor suffered when he came across them. At a follow-up at three months he had continued to progress.

Further reading

Dickson, A. (1982). *A Woman in your Own Right. Assertiveness and You.* London: Quartet Books. [Looks at why women are unassertive, and at the rights of all humans. Practical ideas on how to be assertive as a positive alternative to being manipulative or aggressive. Written for women, but much of it could be useful to men.]

Lucas, M., Wilson, K., and Hart, E. (1986). *How to Survive the 9 to 5.* London: Thames Methuen. [Cheap paperback. Helps you examine your stress at work, and gives suggestions on how to cope with it.]

Madders, J. (1979). *Stress and Relaxation: self-help ways to cope with stress and relieve nervous tension.* London: Martin Dunitz. [Well-illustrated, easy to read book. Discusses stress and how to overcome it with breathing, relaxation and massage.]

Marks, I. (1978). *Living with Fear.* Maidenhead: McGraw-Hill. [The nature of fears, phobias and rituals. How they are treated, including self-help.]

Merrett, C. (1982). *Relaxation Rules.* Southsea: Minds Eye Books. [By post from Minds Eye Books, 47 Festing Grove, Southsea, PO4 9QB. Booklet which aims to help you identify tension and show you how to be more relaxed throughout the day whatever you're doing.]

Merrett, C., Eveleigh, C. and Fortune, R. (1980). *Why Worry?* Southsea: Minds Eye Books (as above). [A booklet which discusses anxiety and worry. Suggests how to relax, think more realistically, and stop avoiding what makes you anxious.]

MIND *Factsheet 8. Agoraphobia and Other Phobias.* London: MIND. [A leaflet which discusses how phobias start and who is at risk. It looks at help from relatives and friends, professionals and self-help.]

MIND *Factsheet 9. Anxiety.* London: MIND. [Leaflet briefly discusses what anxiety is, and how to tackle it with relaxation, assertion training, medical help, hypnotherapy, talking it out, and self-help.]

Relaxation Tapes

There are a large number of tapes for teaching relaxation, sometimes with other suggestions also for dealing with anxiety and stress. The following tape is reasonably priced and is widely used:

Relax and Enjoy it! by Robert Sharpe, from Lifestyle Training Centre, 23 Abingdon Road, London, W8.

Many local education authorities run adult evening or day classes which include relaxation training. These might be classes on relaxation itself, on meditation, yoga, stress management, or the Health Education Council's 'Look After Yourself' course. Ask at the public library for details.

Relaxation For Living is an organization which teaches relaxation using teachers, tapes, and correspondence. They also sell leaflets on stress and relaxation. The address is: 29 Burwood Park Road, Walton-on-Thames, Surrey, KT12 5LH.

Coming off tranquillizers

A number of people who suffer from anxiety also want to stop taking tranquillizers. The following books might be of use to them.

Haddon, C. (1984) *Women and Tranquillizers.* London: Sheldon Press. [Cheap paperback. Practical and sensible advice on how to come off minor tranquillizers.]

MIND *Tranquillizers: hard facts, hard choices.* MIND special report. [Send s.a.e. to MIND. Presents some of the facts about how many people take minor tranquillizers, some of the problems with and alternatives to these drugs.]

Trickett, S. (1986). *Coming off Tranquillizers.* Wellingborough: Thorsons. [Cheap paperback. A step-by-step plan for how to come off minor tranquillizers written by a nurse who has wide experience in helping people.]

❖   ❖   ❖

EATING PROBLEMS

We need food to give us energy for our activities, protein to repair and build our bodies, and vitamins and minerals to keep us healthy.

Energy values of food are measured in calories. The most common problem people have with eating is that they consume more calories than they need, and so become overweight. Some estimate that as many as 40 per cent of adults are overweight. But there are many more ways in which eating can be a problem.

Anorexia nervosa, commonly and inaccurately called 'the slimmers' disease', seems to be the opposite of eating too much. This condition occurs in about one in every 200 girls between the ages of 16 and 18. The sufferer eats very little and can lose a dangerous amount of weight. Less than 10 per cent of sufferers are boys.

Yet another eating disorder, bulimia nervosa, has hit the headlines recently. Again, this is largely a female problem. The sufferer usually maintains an average weight, but eats huge amounts of food in binges, and then makes herself sick or uses laxatives to control her weight.

Finally, fear of eating in public is another eating problem. We don't know how common this is, but like all eating disorders, it can make people's lives a misery. It can either reflect or result in very low self-esteem. Instead of being a source of nutrition and pleasure, eating has got out of control. Eating and weight control are quite complicated, both psychologically and biologically. There are many different approaches to the problem.

Food: a pleasure or a battle?

There are a large number of easily-available methods for losing weight. The multi-million pound diet industry produces countless special foods, magazines, books, and runs slimming clubs. Unfortunately, many people seem to spend their whole lives dieting, so these products alone are not enough to change permanently their behaviour and attitudes to food. Perhaps if they did, the big businesses would run out of customers. Keeping fit is becoming increasingly popular, and is generally a good idea for people who need to lose weight. Slimming clubs are run in almost every town and village. Many overweight people are referred to the dietician at their local hospital, and are either seen individually or in groups, like Robert Smith whose story is told next. For a small number of very overweight people drastic measures are used, such as wiring up their teeth or operations to remove part of the intestine. However, these approaches cannot teach them new and better eating habits.

A feminist approach to why women have problems with eating and with their weight has been developed by two psychotherapists from the Women's Therapy Centre, Susie Orbach and Louise

Eichenbaum. They believe that women have reasons for being ambivalent about their weight, and that these are related to their role in our society. They will not easily make permanent changes in their attitudes towards themselves, or their eating habits until they have explored their feelings about eating and weight. Information about this approach is given in the booklist.

Robert Smith: SEVERELY OVERWEIGHT

Robert asked his doctor to help him to lose weight. Like many would-be dieters he knew all about diets — he had been on hundreds. Unfortunately he had never managed to change his eating *HABITS* permanently. He joined a weight control class run at the local hospital by a dietitian and a psychologist.

Robert is a 45-year-old ambulance man who lives at home with his wife and teenage daughter. He didn't have a weight problem until joining the ambulance service when he was 30. He then gave up football as he couldn't attend practices regularly. Two years ago he gave up smoking and put on another half stone. He started to eat sweets instead of having a cigarette. The dietitian recommended that Robert should aim to lose about two stone.

A *diary makes the problem clearer*

Before Robert began to change his eating habits, he kept a diary of exactly what he ate for a fortnight. It showed both work days and leisure days and helped to build a clear picture of his eating habits. Robert's eating problems were:

1. Skipping breakfast and then eating snacks all morning because he was still hungry.

2. Irregular meals, partly because of shift work.

3. Chips with every meal.

4. Eating chocolate bars when driving.

5. Eating fry-ups when he had to cook for himself, because it seemed most convenient.

6. Sugar in drinks, totalling at least 12 teaspoons a day.

Eight other adults joined the weight control class, which met for about an hour a week for ten weeks. Robert found it a much more useful approach than the diets he had tried to follow on his own. In the class he had the support of fellow sufferers who were enthusiastic about the changes he made. Eating diaries were analysed in the first class, which allowed Robert to make the list of eating problems shown. Then each problem was discussed in turn, and possible alternatives were suggested. For example, for 'skipping breakfast', the alternatives were:

1. Set alarm 15 minutes earlier, so you can still have your lie in, but you will also have time for a couple of slices of toast spread with low fat spread and yeast extract, and a cup of coffee with sweetener instead of sugar.

2. Take a packed breakfast to eat at work.

3. Persuade someone to bring you breakfast in bed.

4. Lay the table for breakfast before you go to bed at night.

After thinking about how practical each alternative was, Robert chose number 1 on the list. The dietitian gave information on the value of breakfasts, and Robert made a shopping list of a few items he would buy to ring the changes at breakfast. When he left the first class he had written himself some goals for tackling two of his eating problems. During the rest of the classes, he tackled all of his eating problems, setting himself realistic goals after considering the choices he had. He learned about the nutritional and calorific values of foods, and about how to eat well and enjoyably for life, rather than 'going on a diet'. He found out about the circumstances in which he tended to eat badly, and what he could do instead. He kept an eating diary throughout. At the end of the ten weeks, Robert was well on the way to his target weight, and was enjoying some of the changes he had made in his eating.

❖ ❖ ❖

Shelley Pope: BULIMIA NERVOSA

Shelley was 24 when she went to her doctor and asked for help with her eating, which she felt had got completely out of control. That weekend she had been shopping for the week's groceries, and when she got home she sat down and ate almost half of them. She felt depressed and terribly guilty afterwards, as usual. She then made herself sick so that she would not put on weight, and to relieve the pain of her over-full stomach. No one else knew about her secret binges, and no one would have guessed because her weight was average for her height and age. That night she read an article in the local paper which described another woman who binged, just like Shelley did.

Finds the courage to ask for help

Like Shelley, the woman in the article had had powerful urges to overeat. She had made herself vomit or had used laxatives to control her weight: she had a terrible fear of becoming fat. She had got over the problem with professional help, and so Shelley plucked up courage to approach her own doctor. She had been increasingly worried about the effects her strange eating patterns might have on her health, and her periods were now irregular. Her voice was always hoarse, which she guessed correctly was due to making herself sick so often. She also risked rotting her teeth with the stomach acids which came through her mouth when she was sick. And on top of feeling miserable about eating and worries about the physical effects on her, Shelley's food bill was enormous. Her social life was limited, as she feared eating with others in case she got out of control and wanted to stuff herself. And she stopped taking part in any sports as she felt uncomfortable about others seeing her in brief sports gear, or in the changing rooms.

Shelley started having her secret feasts alone in the evenings when she first left home to go to university. At first she would buy a large bar of chocolate, and found she couldn't just eat some of it, but had to finish the lot. She wasn't particularly worried, as she knew other people who did the same. But she began to eat other foods uncontrollably, and these sessions became more frequent until they were five or six times a week. She managed to keep them secret from her flat mates, and felt too guilty to tell anyone.

The doctor refers

Shelley's doctor gave her a physical check-up and discussed her mood and eating problems with her at length before referring her on to a clinical psychologist. It was particularly important for her to see a doctor first, as bulimia can result in medical problems. Depression occurs in about 10 per cent of sufferers, and this needs to be treated, possibly with antidepressant drugs, before work on eating can start.

Psychological treatment

For the first month Shelley saw the psychologist twice a week for about 50 minutes. They worked together on changing her eating habits. They worked out an eating plan which included three good meals a day plus two or three snacks, and Shelley wrote this down. Even though she had been vomiting her food she could not have got rid of it all this way. She would have digested about one third of it. So it seemed logical to her to eat that food in the form of enjoyable meals. At this stage she was just eating food that she enjoyed, to get back into the habit of regular meals. She planned what to do after meals, so that she wouldn't be tempted to go on eating. Until now, Shelley had been weighing herself twice a day. To teach her to be less preoccupied with her weight, she agreed to weigh herself only once a week.

For the second and third month, Shelley saw the psychologist once a week. Now that she was eating regular meals and not vomiting, she started to eat well-balanced meals. This meant eating some of the foods she had been frightened to eat in case they would start her off on an uncontrollable binge. She also spent a lot of time with the psychologist looking at her thoughts, her beliefs and her values about food and about herself. Some of these had helped cause her eating problem in the first place. She kept a diary of her thoughts about eating. For example, when offered a biscuit Shelley said to herself: 'I daren't take one or I'll have to eat the lot and they'll think I'm a pig. But they'll think I'm funny if I refuse'. No wonder she had some uncomfortable feelings about food. Now she can say to herself: 'Do I really fancy one? I don't have to have one just to seem polite. I'm entitled to say no'. And if she *does* want one: 'I'll just have one because I'm not really hungry. I've had just one before, enjoyed it and felt really pleased with myself. I can imagine feeling really pleased with myself this time too'. Shelley and the psychologist used the diary to question her thoughts about eating, so she learned to give herself appropriate and helpful answers.

For the last few sessions, Shelley saw the psychologist once every fortnight. She used this time to plan ahead so that she could continue with the gains she had made when she no longer had the psychologist's support. She discussed how she would cope with any foreseeable problems, and how she would spend all the extra time and money that she had freed for herself by learning to eat well. She found this planning very useful, but she realised that eating itself was not her only problem. Instead, it was her way of coping with other problems and feelings, and it had got out of hand.

Further reading

French, B. (1987). *Coping with Bulimia.* Wellingborough: Thorsons. [Describes the 'binge–purge' syndrome in detail, and its side-effects. Includes a self-help plan for recovery.]

Orbach, S. (1978). *Fat is a Feminist Issue . . . the anti-diet guide to permanent weight loss.* London: Hamlyn. [Looks at why women have problems with eating and weight. Includes case histories and psychological exercises which can be used alone or in a group.]

Orbach, S. (1982). *Fat is a Feminist Issue II . . . A practical book/tape programme to conquer compulsive eating.* London: Hamlyn. [A self-help guide to changing compulsive eating patterns.]

Slade, R. (1984). *The Anorexia Nervosa Reference Book.* London: Harper and Row. [Straightforward and detailed account of the progress and prognosis of the disorder. In particular, it examines the underlying attitudes and beliefs of the anorexic.]

SEXUAL PROBLEMS

Apparently we live in an age of sexual openness and freedom, but despite this (or in some cases because of it) a lot of people, both men and women, still have sexual difficulties, such as not having any interest in sex, not getting sexually aroused, and not experiencing a climax. Many of these difficulties are short-lived, and may be related to ill health, or some kind of stress in life or in the relationship. In themselves, they are not a problem if the people concerned are quite happy, and it's nobody else's business. One study of 100 happily-married couples found that 80 per cent described their marital and sexual relations as happy and satisfying. But, despite this, nearly half the men, and over half the women had sexual difficulties. Such difficulties can affect other sides of the relationship. If either partner is concerned, there are a number of sources of help that one or both of them can turn to.

Specialist help

In some health districts there are specialist sex therapy clinics. Many of these are staffed by psychiatrists, but they might also include other doctors, clinical psychologists, social workers and nurse therapists. In places where there is no specialist clinic there may be individual professionals with a special interest or special training in helping people with sexual problems. Some gynaecologists specialize in this area. Usually your GP will be able to refer you. Family planning clinic staff also advise people on sexual difficulties. The Marriage Guidance Council has people trained in sex therapy. You can go to them directly, without a letter from your GP. They're in *The Phone Book* under 'M'.

Some sex therapists work in pairs, so if you go with your partner you will see both a male and a female therapist. Many sex therapists use an approach based on relearning how to give and receive sexual pleasure, such as that devised by the American therapists William Masters and Virginia Johnson, or Helen Kaplan. Others use a more psychodynamic approach and focus on underlying conflicts, both between the sexual partners, and in other significant relationships. Sex therapy is for anyone with a sexual problem, heterosexual or homosexual, with a partner or not.

Carol and Phil Stewart:
OVERCOMING SEXUAL DIFFICULTIES

Carol and Phil had been married for four years. To start with, they had been very happy together. Their reasons for being together were as good as they had ever been. But for about the last two years they had begun not to talk to each other much, and were both increasingly unhappy. They made love less and less often. When they did make love, neither of them enjoyed it much any more, although they never talked to each other about this. One night Phil approached Carol to make love, and she burst out crying. They were both very distressed by Carol's reaction, and as they still loved each other, they began to talk about things they were unhappy about. The conversation wasn't easy, and they said some pretty hurtful things to each other that they had been bottling up. But the good thing was that they both agreed that they had a problem with sex, and that they wanted to get help for it.

Confronting their problem

Carol had seen a magazine article about sex therapy which said you could ask your GP to refer you to an NHS sex therapy clinic. It explained how when sex becomes a problem, it can affect the relationship in many ways and get quite out of proportion. Whereas good sex, although lovely and worthwhile, is not the be-all and end-all. To sum up this idea: 'Bad sex is 90 per cent of a relationship, but good sex is only 10 per cent of a relationship'. In other words, when you are unhappy about sex, it can seem to take over your life. But when it is good, it is only a small though important part of your relationship. Carol and Phil agreed that the problem was getting out of hand, and they couldn't cope with it by themselves. So they went to see their GP together. At first they both felt very embarrassed, but it turned out that their GP was specially trained to help people with sexual problems, and she soon put them at their ease. She suggested that Carol and Phil should visit her each week for a special 40-minute appointment outside surgery times, so that they would have plenty of time to discuss the problems and what to do about them. In all, they went eight times.

The GP helps

The GP didn't seem at all uncomfortable discussing sex. She wasn't shocked or surprised by anything, and didn't mind that they used their own words for parts of the body or activities, when they either didn't know or feel comfortable with the medical words. They agreed that the first long meeting was just to agree on the actual problem, or problems. This sounds easier than it was. It turned out that both Carol and Phil had their own problems, and that these problems affected each other. That was why things had got worse over the last two years.

Carol had *never* had an orgasm during love-making. Although she used to find sex exciting, she took a long time to get turned on. Recently she found she wasn't getting turned on at all. When they had sexual intercourse, Carol liked to get it over as quickly as possible, because she felt physically uncomfortable and emotionally distant. She had never talked openly about her feelings to do with sex, or told Phil what she liked or didn't like.

Phil too found it difficult to talk about his feelings about sex. He had always felt that sexual intercourse lasted too short a time, but couldn't make himself last longer. He didn't have many ideas about how to turn Carol on, and had given up trying most of the time as he usually got such a disappointing response.

They agreed that they both wanted to learn to talk more openly about their sexual feelings, their needs, likes and dislikes. Carol wanted to learn how to have an orgasm, and Phil wanted to learn how to last longer during intercourse. Technically speaking, Carol was pre-orgasmic or anorgasmic. (The word 'frigid' used to be used, but many therapists have now dropped this term with its negative associations.) Phil suffered from premature ejaculation.

Working at home

Once they had all agreed what the problems were, and what they wanted to achieve, the treatment included homework exercises in communication and in building up their sex life from the start again. The GP said that Carol and Phil should not have sexual intercourse until she said so. Once this pressure was off them they both felt much more relaxed and began to enjoy their 'homework'. At first it seemed strange and contrived having to specially make time for the home-work. They both wanted their love life to be natural and spontaneous, but they agreed that it was worth doing the homework, however awkward they felt. After all, they were both in the same boat.

They looked at how to 'set the scene' and make time for their love life. The homework tasks included ways of getting to know their own and the other's body and talking about their bodies. They spent time touching, massaging and caressing each other, first avoiding the sexual parts. This helped them to get pleasure from the other person's enjoyment, as well as learn what felt good for themselves and for their partner. Then they were given tasks for Carol to learn how to have an orgasm, first by masturbating alone, and then by showing Phil what felt good. The GP suggested the 'stop-start' technique for Phil to learn how to last longer during intercourse. This was similar to Carol's exercises, in that first he masturbated alone, and then showed Carol how to do it for him. The difference was that as soon as he felt he was about to reach the point of no return and ejaculate, Carol stopped stimulating him.

A new approach

When they actually started having intercourse again, they spent much longer on the preliminaries than previously. Their homework had helped Carol and Phil to talk more openly and constructively to each other. They both enjoyed all aspects of their sex life together, not only intercourse. Carol began to have orgasms during intercourse, usually when she or Phil gave her added stimulation by hand. Sometimes she didn't have an orgasm, but she still enjoyed herself and neither of them worried. Phil used the 'stop-start' during intercourse itself when necessary. They also learned to use a painless squeeze technique to stop him coming to orgasm too soon. This involves stopping intercourse and withdrawing, then firmly squeezing a particular place at the head of the penis with a thumb and two fingers.

Carol and Phil had learned a lot about sex, and about themselves and each other. They felt much closer.

Further reading

Brown, P. and Faulder, C. (1979). *Treat Yourself to Sex: a guide to good loving.* Harmondsworth: Penguin. [Cheap paperback. Using 'sex-pieces', the authors suggest ways you can enhance your sex life and overcome sexual problems.]

❖ ❖ ❖

PSYCHOLOGICAL CARE IN SOME COMMON MEDICAL CONDITIONS: a new specialism

▽ *Gemma Davies: learning to live with diabetes.*
▽ *Edna Phillips: chronic pain.*
▽ *Bill Needham: after a stroke.*

The case histories up to now cover what are perhaps more obvious psychological problems. But very often psychological difficulties accompany medical problems. Recently psychologists' interest in behavioural medicine, as it is called, has grown but it is still a very small specialism in British clinical psychology. The next three cases look at people with common medical conditions and at aspects of the psychological care involved: Gemma Davies has diabetes, Edna Phillips suffers chronic pain, and Bill Needham has had a stroke. But first, we look at one example of behavioural medicine in action: research into diabetes.

The work in diabetes is a good example of how psychological approaches to the problems of physical illness can improve people's well-being, sometimes physical as well as psychological. Only a small amount of psychologists' work in diabetes is directly with individuals such as Gemma. Much of the work is concerned with research.

Psychological research in diabetes

Psychologists have been involved in research to try and understand why some people with diabetes find it easier to look after themselves than do others. They have looked at the knowledge and beliefs of diabetics and how this affects their metabolic control, as they can become ill if they eat the wrong foods or at the wrong times, or overdo exercise which can cause extreme levels of blood sugar. Psychologists also research the attitudes and behaviour of the professionals involved. They have found that people need more than accurate knowledge about coping with diabetes in order to cope well.

If people believe that there is great value in looking after themselves, they are more likely to look after themselves well. People with diabetes do better if they can see some benefits for themselves in managing their diabetes. This could mean seeing that life would be more trouble-free, or that they could avoid hypos (caused by mistimed or wrong eating, or perhaps too much exercise).

Some people believe that looking after their diabetes is much too difficult and embarrassing, and that it would interfere too much with their life to take it seriously. It might be that these people do worse in looking after themselves. People who admit that they have difficulties in managing their diabetes, who are actually facing up to the problems, are the ones who tend to do well in terms of metabolic control.

Who is responsible for managing diabetes? Is successful metabolic control achieved by the actions of the person with diabetes, or the actions of the professional? Or just by pure luck? The way both the person with diabetes and their health professional think about these questions will very much influence the way they get on together. If professionals are not careful, they can unwittingly undermine the efforts of people to care for themselves. Some psychologists are researching the attitudes and behaviour of professionals, and teaching them consultation skills, such as how to listen to people.

Further reading

Sönksen, P., Fox, C., and Judd, S. (1985). *The Diabetes Reference Book.* London: Harper & Row. [Gives clear answers to very many questions asked by people with diabetes.]

Gemma Davis: LEARNING TO LIVE WITH DIABETES

About one person in every 50 in England has diabetes. It is much rarer in children, with only one child in 500. Gemma's diabetes was first diagnosed when she was 24 years old. Four years later, she first met a clinical psychologist when she attended an information group for people with diabetes. The information group helped her to develop the skills of looking after herself, so that she could achieve good metabolic control. The group was run by the diabetes staff at the general hospital. Any staff who could help attended at one time or another: nurses, doctors, a dietitian, a chiropodist and the psychologist. Gemma was very well informed about diabetes and how to cope with it. She scored one of the top marks on a questionnaire which measured her knowledge. She got her diabetes under very good control, but she still felt terrible about having diabetes at all. So she went to see the psychologist.

Low self-confidence

Gemma is an intelligent woman who had been very cheerful and ambitious before discovering her diabetes, but now developed a very low opinion of herself. She had a responsible position in a large company and had hoped to develop her career, now she no longer felt she was worthy of promotion. She was stuck in the same job, even though she was capable of doing more. She felt her boss was protecting her from the work, and giving her less and less to do. She now felt as if she was a second class citizen, and not good enough for her boyfriend. She often felt moody, anxious, upset and depressed. To look at, she seemed very tense. She was terribly upset about having diabetes and needed to come to terms with it. She couldn't face going out socially. She wouldn't go out with her boyfriend any more, and they just met in her home.

Working on a new view

The psychologist usually saw Gemma with her boyfriend. They worked together on Gemma's negative view of herself. She thought diabetes had ruined her life. Her expectations had changed completely, and she would say things like: 'If it wasn't for my diabetes, I would be able to go sailing'. In fact, the only thing that stopped her from going sailing was her own attitude. She often thought about the dreadful catastrophes that might occur to her because of the diabetes, and these worries had got completely out of proportion. She learned to see that she was often limiting herself unnecessarily. Using cognitive methods, she learned to be much more realistic and positive about herself and her diabetes. She began to look at the evidence that she was doing well. Looking after herself well became a source of pleasure for her. She had a sense of being in charge again. She also practised a method of relaxation. With the psychologist, she set goals for things she would do, like going out socially, and began to enjoy a more fulfilling life. Her more positive attitude was rewarded at work when she got promoted.

❖   ❖   ❖

Edna Phillips: CHRONIC PAIN

Edna had had low back pain for ten years, and many full medical examinations and tests had found no reason for it. Now in her 40's, she had had treatment from an osteopath and from a pain clinic, but with no lasting benefit. She also suffered from depression and anxiety, and had seen a psychiatrist for several years. She had given up her job, and now hardly did anything for herself or around the house. Her husband and their grown-up son looked after her. She spent most of her time worrying that she had an undetected tumour, and that she would soon be dead. Her own mother had died from a tumour.

Edna's GP referred her to a psychologist, hoping that Edna would be helped to change the way she viewed her pain. Her attitude towards the pain was more of a handicap than the pain itself. The psychologist had seen many people who had pain for which there was no medical cause or treatment.

The first interview was to get a clear picture of what the pain was like and how it affected her life and that of her family. At first, Edna seemed very agitated and upset. She was disappointed that the first interview did not give her a solution to the problem. She generally felt angry and powerless about her problem, and her lack of control over her life. She believed that she might die before her second appointment the following week.

Assessing the impact of pain

The first interview was at Edna's own home. The psychologist asked detailed questions about when the pain first started, when it occurred, if it was ever better or worse, and how Edna viewed it. He asked her to fill in a questionnaire about her pain. They also looked at what the pain stopped her from doing, what she did less often because of her pain, and what she would most like to do if the pain went. These answers helped the psychologist and Edna to work out a programme of activities at later meetings, which helped Edna to get the most out of her life in spite of the pain.

It turned out that Edna could only cope with the pain by taking tablets and lying down. She had stopped doing the housework, going shopping, playing darts, and even bathing alone. Her family had rallied round, and now did all the housework, shopping and cooking. She wanted to be able to look after herself, and follow her own interests.

Treatment

The psychologist saw Edna once a week for ten weeks, then once a fortnight for five meetings, then monthly for six months. The first meetings lasted an hour, but later ones were down to 30 and then 20 minutes. At first, the psychologist visited her at home, but after two months Edna was able to come to the clinic alone. At some of their meetings, Edna's husband and son joined in. The psychologist appreciated that Edna's pain was real and not imaginary, although no medical reason had been found for it despite all the tests.

They agreed that their goal was to help her make the most of her life, despite the pain. To illustrate the importance of this in helping Edna to cope with her pain, the psychologist used an example from his own life. He had a severe headache and was walking through the town. His head was thumping. Along his walk he had to cross a busy road, where he needed to concentrate on the traffic. When he got to the other side, he noticed his headache 'come back'. That did not mean he did not have a headache for the minute or so that he was crossing the road. Rather, because he was distracted by something else, he did not notice the pain. Edna thought this was a good example of the way things sometimes happened with her pain. Just because the pain seemed to go it did not mean it had been in her imagination. But it did mean that getting involved in something else could help her live better with the pain.

In the first week, Edna kept a diary of everything she did, using a chart like the one shown. She also recorded how bad the pain was. At first her life looked very empty. With the psychologist she made a plan

Pain Record: MONDAY

Time	Circumstances	Pain (0-10)	Comments
8 - 9AM	Woke up. Tea in bed. Listened to radio. Husband asked if I'd be alright.	4	Same as usual.
9 - 9.30AM	Dozed.	?	
9.30AM	Phone rang. Cousin asked me to a party. Refused the pain would spoil it for me.	7	
9.45	Turned on T.V. Lay on sofa.	6	Bored. Lay down to cope with pain.
10.00	Watched birds feeding outside the window.	3	How interesting!
10.30	Alice called for a chat and made us some coffee.	3-4	Alice is a comic. She brings me out of myself.

each week of the things that she wanted to do. She planned at least one small activity for each morning, afternoon and evening. This included getting up to join her family for breakfast, wearing her dressing gown, and doing one small cleaning job in the house each morning. She then recorded on her activity plan what she had actually done. Sometimes Edna's pain seemed to be worse because she was tense, so as well as increasing her activities, Edna learned progressive relaxation. She looked at whether she had anything to lose by learning to cope with the pain and living a fuller life. It would drastically change her relationship with her family and the things they did for each other. She also agreed with her family that she would talk to them about her activities, and not complain about the pain all the time. These issues were discussed at several meetings before she was able to do anything about them.

After a month or so of working out her activity plans with the psychologist, Edna did them on her own, and then discussed them with the psychologist at their sessions. Although her general progress was in the right direction, she suffered some relapses on the way, when she did less for herself. Eventually, she greatly increased the number of things she did, and could get pleasure from. The pain did not stop her. After a few months she and her husband asked for some guidance on improving their sex life, as this had been restricted for some years.

Further reading

Broome, A. and Jellicoe, H. (1987). *Living with Your Pain.* Leicester: The British Psychological Society & Methuen. [A self-help guide to living with chronic pain.]

Peck, C. (1985 rev. ed.) *Controlling Chronic Pain. A self-help guide.* London: Fontana. [A cheap paperback which helps a person with chronic pain to look at the way pain limits their life, and then gives step-by-step instructions, using worksheets and charts, for increasing activity, and solving problems including depression.]

❖ ❖ ❖

Bill Needham: AFTER A STROKE

Bill, aged 50, was taken into his local general hospital after a stroke: a blood vessel in his brain had leaked. He was one of the 100,000 people in the UK who suffer from a stroke every year. A stroke can cause very complicated problems, such as with memory, speech, dressing or looking after yourself, and walking. And it can make any existing psychological and relationship problems worse, by the strain it puts on the people involved. People respond very differently to strokes. In Bill's case he could still talk normally, but he could not walk at first. He was often disorientated, and sometimes did not recognize his son or called his wife 'mother'. The hospital had a rehabilitation centre and Bill was sent there.

The hospital team

The rehabilitation team was led by a consultant in rehabilitation and included other doctors, occupational therapists, physiotherapists, speech therapists, a social worker and a part-time psychologist. Not all such teams include a psychologist. The psychologist's contribution was advising and supporting staff and families, more than assessing or treating the patients. Together, the work of the team was to assess how each patient would be affected by the stroke, and to help them return to as normal a life as possible. This might include teaching them how to walk again, or how to be as independent as possible in a wheelchair. It could also involve helping patients' families to cope with the changes.

Bill saw each member of the rehabilitation team separately so they could assess the effects of the stroke. He was feeling tired and depressed, so these meetings were brief. The doctors had various tests done on him, including a brain scan and an EEG (although these particular tests are not routine for stroke patients). The psychologist asked Bill a lot of questions, and also gave him tests which involved writing, drawing and rearranging small objects. The tests were to assess his memory, and to help predict how much he would be able to get out of rehabilitation. Then the team met to agree a plan for Bill's treatment.

Rehabilitation

Most of Bill's rehabilitation was in the form of occupational therapy and physiotherapy. After about a month he was discharged home, but came back every day by ambulance to continue his rehabilitation as an outpatient. He then saw the psychologist again; he was feeling guilty and depressed about the effect he was having on the family. His wife came with him on some visits, as they both wanted to discuss their worries about resuming their sex life. Bill's wife was a great support to him. She attended a stroke group for relatives at the centre, which gave them support and also information about strokes from different rehabilitation professionals. There was lots of time for questions and discussion. Some of the stroke patients attended a group run by the psychologist to help them with memory problems. Here, they learned and practised strategies to help them cope with the problems of having a poor memory. Bill's memory was not badly affected, so he did not need to attend the group.

Further reading

Langon Hewer, R. and Wade, D.T. (1986). *Stroke: A practical guide towards recovery.* London: Dunitz. [A well-illustrated cheap paperback which covers topics from 'What is a stroke?' to coping with the effects of a stroke, both immediately and in the longer term.]

❖   ❖   ❖

4. Different Approaches To Therapy

▽ *A counselling approach.*
▽ *A behavioural approach.*
▽ *Cognitive therapy.*
▽ *A psychodynamic approach.*
▽ *Family therapy.*

The traditional psychiatric way of looking at emotional and behavioural problems is to use a 'medical model'. This treats the person rather as if their body and mind are a complicated machine. If something goes wrong the doctors look for the 'faulty part' and try to fix it. They often do this by giving drugs that act on the part of the brain which seems to be functioning badly. (Or they might use psychoanalysis which aims to find and change a problematic part of the personality.) Undoubtedly there are biological changes and illnesses which can result in psychological problems, and drugs can play a very useful part in helping some people. But the focus of this book is on psychological approaches to treatment that do not rely on drugs. Drugs might still play a part, however. For example, some cases of depression are best helped with a combination of anti-depressant drugs and a psychological approach.

Not everyone treating people with psychological problems works in the same way. This is largely because, through their training, they have different ways of viewing the problems, or use different approaches to understand why problems occur. For example, one therapist might see that problems are caused by faulty learning, so the solution is to help the person learn a new response. Another might understand the same kind of problem to be due to upsets early on in a person's life which they need to come to terms with. So this therapist would encourage the person to discuss their early bad experiences, re-experience the upset, and so be able to put it right behind them at last. The choice of therapy is all about matching the person to the approach. In other words, finding the approach and the therapist with which the individual feels happiest. As well as the approach they use and their training, the way a therapist works will be influenced by the time available. It will also depend on their own preferences, their personal strengths and weaknesses, and what they feel comfortable doing.

Therapists might describe each other as:

'He's a cognitive-behaviourist.'

'She looks at problems using a medical model.'

'She's into analytic psychotherapy.'

All of these describe therapists of different schools of thought, who have a different basic understanding or theory of how people develop. Each school of thought has its own theory as to how problems arise, and each has its own ways of treating people with problems. So too each has its own vocabulary to describe and make sense of people, their development, behaviour, experiences and relationships with others. There are many different approaches to psychological problems and types of psychological therapy. This chapter briefly outlines some of those you might come across in the NHS. In practice, most therapists are eclectic and use a number of different approaches, choosing the approach to suit the individual. Some use different approaches for different problems.

► A COUNSELLING APPROACH ◄

What kind of person would you want to talk to if you were extremely distressed? Have you ever unburdened yourself to a friend or professional and thought afterwards: 'I found it much easier to talk than I had expected. They really seemed to understand'. What kind of person did you talk to, and what did they do? Do you know a good listener? What do they do that tells you they are listening? Spend a few minutes thinking about these questions, before reading the rest of this section. Your answers to these questions may show some of the personal qualities and skills needed in a counsellor.

More and more people have some sort of training in counselling, both professionals and people involved in self-help and voluntary work. So what is it? According to dictionaries, to counsel means to advise, to recommend or to consult. The counselling approach to helping people with psychological problems is far from any of these. It is worth starting by saying what counselling is NOT. It is NOT just a friendly chat. NOR is it giving advice unless factual information is needed. It is NOT the counsellor imposing their opinions and values on the other person. It is NOT about the counsellor making decisions for the client, but rather about helping clients make decisions for themselves. The British Association for Counselling says that 'the task is to give the client an opportunity to explore, discover and clarify ways of living more resourcefully and towards greater well-being'.

The counselling relationship should foster trust and understanding, and give clients some space to express themselves. One of the basic counselling skills is *listening.* Counsellors are skilled listeners who can find out what is behind the client's words by attending to the whole person. Not just the words, but also the tone of voice, the body language, and any inconsistencies between what is said and the feelings conveyed. Counsellors give accurate feedback to clients about what they have said or the impression they have given. This feedback helps clients to organize their thoughts and make sense of muddles.

A skilled counsellor not only provides a warm and safe environment for the client to talk, but can help the person be specific, and make difficult decisions for themselves, or come to terms with unpleasant feelings and experiences. Counselling is used as a therapy in its own right, or it can be one phase of therapy in which a number of helping techniques are used.

► A BEHAVIOURAL APPROACH ◄

This is a relatively new approach which has been available for about 25 years. At first it was mostly used by clinical psychologists, but its use has now spread to many other mental health professionals. Behavioural treatments grew out of experiments about how animals and humans learn, and the effectiveness of behavioural treatment methods is well-researched. The approach takes the view that the problems people have which are called 'neurotic' are not due to some kind of illness but to faulty *learning.*

For example, someone with a phobia of cats, like John Sidman (pages 21-23), might have learned to be terrified of them either because of a nasty experience with a cat in the past, or because they had the example of someone who was important to them being afraid of cats. That person might have unintentionally taught them to flap and panic when confronting cats. The fear would have continued because the person then avoided cats and never had the chance to learn to approach them. The way to overcome a problem due to faulty learning is to learn a new and more helpful response as John did. Setting goals of practical tasks, and usually carrying out some of these as homework, is central to a behavioural approach.

When behaviour therapy was new, behaviour therapists were only interested in what could be observed: what people did or said. In recent years, there has been a flourishing of interest in how people's thoughts, beliefs and values affect their behaviour. Together these are known as 'cognitions', and provide the focus of a cognitive approach to therapy.

► COGNITIVE THERAPY ◄

The cognitive therapist says that thoughts influence feelings and behaviour which in turn influence thoughts again, like a circle. So you can get in to a negative circle, where negative thoughts give rise to negative feelings and unhelpful behaviour. These negative thoughts are automatic, as in the examples given of John Sidman and Shelley Pope. You don't deliberately create them. The aim of cognitive therapy is to identify these negative automatic thoughts and help the person question them and answer them with more useful and realistic thoughts. That way the person can learn to think more constructively, then feel better, and change their behaviour.

All of us talk to ourselves in our heads much of the time. Sometimes this is like a running commentary of what is going on, or what might happen. Sometimes our immediate thoughts are in full sentences like: 'I bet no one speaks to me if I go to that party alone'. Or they may be in the form of pictures of what might happen, like a film. We sometimes say quite literally; 'I can just picture myself in that situation'. Our thoughts can be helpful, such as when we congratulate ourselves for having a go at something. For example, after the first, nerve-wracking driving lesson. Being positive and congratulating yourself may help you feel good and make it more likely you will have another go. Thoughts can sometimes be neither helpful or harmful. Or they can actually be harmful if they add to us feeling lousy, and stop us from getting on with life. For example, the man who thought no one would speak to him at a party might have not gone, and just stayed at home feeling miserable and lonely, thinking about how few people he knew and what a terrible social life he had. Whereas if he had gone to the party, he might have had a good time and made some friends. It was a risk, but if he didn't go at all there was no chance of meeting anyone.

► A PSYCHODYNAMIC APPROACH ◄

Most people have heard of Sigmund Freud, the father of psychoanalysis. He lived from 1865 to 1939, and had a huge impact on approaches to emotional difficulties as well as to the arts. In his lifetime, his ideas were quite revolutionary. His Victorian contemporaries were shocked by his openness about sex, and the way he tried to understand apparently unrelated problems in terms of sexual drives or deep-seated needs. These days, there are many different approaches to 'talking treatments' which are in some way based on Freud's original ideas. Freud's kind of therapy, psychoanalysis, can take place over several years, with therapist and patient meeting several times each week. The therapies which have since developed from psychoanalysis, the (psycho)dynamic (psycho)therapies, usually involve fewer meetings than this. Therapy might be quite short term, involving perhaps only a few meetings of one hour, once a week. Or a person might stay in therapy for over a year.

Unlike behavioural or cognitive therapies, psychodynamic therapies are particularly concerned with the unconscious; that is, unacceptable wishes, feelings and memories linked with our pasts, which we are not normally aware of, but which are thought to be the root of current problems. Following this school of thought, the apparent problem is only a symptom of something deeper. It is seen as the result of feelings unacceptable to the person, that cannot be acknowledged or expressed, because they remind them of something too distressing in the past. Although the therapist wants to remove 'the symptom', the main aim is to help the person change in a more profound way. This can be seen as removing obstacles to growing and maturing as a human being.

The therapist and client look as if they are having a conversation. Therapists do not try to solve their clients' problems, but try to help them understand themselves from the inside.

There are many 'defence mechanisms' all of us use to cope with unacceptable ideas. These include denial, where we appear to completely forget an unpleasant experience, and projection, where we see what is unacceptable about ourselves in someone else. Sometimes discussing dreams can help to bring something important to the surface. Freud called dreams the 'royal road to the unconscious'. He saw dreaming as a way of solving problems, fulfilling wishes, or coping with unpleasant experiences.

The relationship between the therapist and client is central. It can be seen like a mirror, which reflects and repeats other important relationships in the life of the client. So clients might react in a similar way to their therapists as they did, for example, to their fathers. This is known as transference, as clients transfer to therapists their attitudes and feelings about other people. By pointing out what is going on between themselves and their clients, therapists help their clients to understand such significant relationships. Therapists listen carefully and offer interpretations, to make sense of and make links between what is said.

Many of the other forms of psychotherapy or 'talking treatments' have grown out of psychoanalytic ideas. Some of these are grouped together under the umbrella term 'humanistic psychotherapies'. These include TRANSACTIONAL ANALYSIS, GESTALT THERAPY and PSYCHODRAMA. These may be available free under the NHS if there is a local therapist with particular expertise in them.

Transactional analysis is a system of therapy normally used in a group. It looks at the way people relate to each other, each from the 'parent', 'adult' or 'child' part of themselves.

Gestalt therapy concentrates on what is going on in the present, and on becoming aware of our feelings, bodies, actions and choices.

In *psychodrama* you act out situations and conflicts which disturb you, usually in a group.

CO-COUNSELLING is very much a self-help approach developed from the psychoanalytic school. In it, people pair up together, learn together, and take it in turns to counsel one another. People do not spend so long in those forms of therapy as in traditional psychoanalysis.

► **FAMILY THERAPY** ◄

Family therapy, as the name implies, offers help to whole families and not just individuals. it concentrates on the relationships between people, rather than on the individuals themselves. A family therapy approach sees that when one member of a family seems to have a particular emotional problem, every one in the family is in some way involved. A problem experienced by a family member might have many causes, and may affect each member in some way. Therapists are not looking for someone to blame. They want to help the family to communicate and to find a way to solve the problems.

Therapists usually like to see all the members of the immediate family. Some therapists will also want to include other people who play a large part in the family life, such as a lodger, or a grandmother who lives nearby. Often it is the child who is first referred for help for something like school refusal, soiling or stealing. Sometimes a whole family is offered therapy when one of the parents has the obvious problem, such as when a mother is agoraphobic, or when a father drinks too much.

The staff of child and family guidance units usually practise family therapy, as do staff in specialized family therapy centres. The professionals involved are child psychiatrists, social workers, nurses, clinical and educational psychologists and occupational therapists. There may be one or two therapists to a family.

In some clinics, particularly where some of the staff are in training, the sessions may be watched by staff in another room, using a one-way mirror or video. This would only be allowed with the family's consent. The purpose of the other staff is partly to allow more people to contribute to sorting out the problems: the 'watchers' may notice things that the therapists miss. It also can help in training new therapists. The therapy room may have toys and paints, so that the children can behave as naturally as possible.

There are several types of family therapy, and all are relatively new (that is, less than 25 years old). Three of the main types are based on psychodynamic theory, behavioural theory, and general systems theory. A brief introduction to behavioural and psychodynamic approaches to therapy was given earlier in this chapter. In the last approach, systems theory, therapists are particularly interested in the groups or subsystems within the family and how they work. For example, how the parents work together on their tasks of looking after the family, in terms of emotional support, giving time to the children and to each other, and agreeing on and applying discipline. The therapists might want to discuss how when one parent is particularly soft the other becomes more strict, to keep some kind of discipline among the children. The children also form a subsystem, doing things together. There may also be other subsystems, such as the mother and eldest daughter who pal up together and somehow keep out the father.

Therapy involves a lot of talking, but often the family is involved more actively as well. Some family therapists start by asking about the family's history, so that they can draw their recent family tree. The family tree can even include pets, who may be very important members of the family. Talking about the family tree can help to bring out such things as deaths or breakups in the family which some members have never been able to discuss, and which still upset them very much. Therapists might ask a family to run through situations which they found difficult in the past, to help them understand what was going on, and find different ways of handling them in future. And very often the therapist gives a family a task to do as homework.

Further reading

Clare, A. and Thompson, S. (1981). *Let's Talk About Me. A critical examination of the new psychotherapies.* London: British Broadcasting Corporation. [Looks at many of the newer psychotherapies and asks 'What do they do?' 'Do they work', and 'Are they harmful?']

MIND *Factsheet 6. Talking Treatments.* London: MIND. [This leaflet introduces the would-be client to what can be expected from various forms of psychotherapy or counselling, and looks at possible problems with talking treatments.]

5. Who Can Help With A Psychological Problem?

▽ *Clinical psychologist.* ▽ *Psychiatrist.*
▽ *Community psychiatric nurse.* ▽ *Nurse therapist.*
▽ *Mental health social workers.* ▽ *MIND worker.*
▽ *General practitioner.* ▽ *Alcohol counsellor.*
▽ *Marriage guidance counsellor.* ▽ *Student counsellor.*
▽ *Qualifications.*

Do you already know someone who might help?

For many people the GP is the first (and often the only) person they discuss a problem with. Your GP may have a special interest and expertise in helping with your kind of problem, and may be able to give you all the help you need (see pages 66–67). Usually you need to see a GP in order to get referred on to one of the other professionals mentioned in this chapter. The GP will know, or be able to find out, exactly what services are available locally and how long you are likely to have to wait for an appointment. Alternatively, if you are already seeing another professional, like a health visitor or social worker, you may like to discuss the problem with them.

Voluntary organizations and self-help groups

You may find there is a voluntary organization or self-help group which can help you. Some people prefer this to seeing a professional, or use this as well as seeing a professional; or they might be referred there by their GP or health visitor. MIND and the National Marriage Guidance Council are two of the main ones. MIND is the major voluntary mental health organization in England and Wales. They employ professionals as well as volunteers, and can provide a wide range of help to people in distress and their families. There is more about one MIND worker on pages 64–65. Local branches of MIND sometimes also give advice to self-help groups.

Marriage Guidance Counsellors will see people with psychological problems, as well as those with obvious relationship difficulties. For more about the work of a Marriage Guidance Counsellor, see page 70.

Self-help groups are on the increase and deal with all kinds of problems. For example, some women's health groups organize self-help meetings for women with eating disorders, such as bulimia nervosa, or for people coming off tranquillizers. To find out more about what is available locally, ask at the Citizen's Advice Bureau or library. The library might also stock two useful reference books: *Someone To Talk To Directory 1985: a directory of self-help and community support agencies in the UK and the Republic of Ireland* (1985, Mental Health Foundation, Routledge & Kegan Paul); and the *Voluntary Agencies Directory* (1987, Harper & Row). These cover health as well as many other topics.

Your local Volunteer Bureau or Council for Voluntary Service may have someone who is a mine of information on self-help groups. They may even know someone whose job it is to assist such groups. Some local newspapers produce a directory of local organizations, or you might try the local radio station.

Other sources of information might be the Community Health Council, or the Health Education Department of your district health authority. A few health education departments operate a 'Healthline' telephone service, as described later. The Samaritans, or local 'Nightline' telephone counselling service may be able to put you in touch with local groups.

Anyone can telephone the 'Healthline' service and ask to hear a tape about a health subject they are interested in, or ask if they know of a particular self-help group. The Health Information Trust runs this service, which has tape recordings of up-to-date information on health topics and health services. There are numerous tapes covering all kinds of topics, some of which contain information on national and local self-help groups. The service is available to anyone by phoning 01-980-4848 between 2pm and 10pm, seven days a week and unlike some private 'phone services, it will only cost you the usual 'phone call. A directory of the tapes is published free and new tapes are being added all the time. For a copy of the Healthline Directory write to: PO Box 499, London E2 9PU, enclosing s.a.e.

Self-help books

There is an ever increasing number of self-help books for all kinds of psychological problems. Some simply provide information about a particular problem; others are more like a manual and suggest a particular step-by-step approach to overcoming the problem. If you see a therapist, he or she might recommend a book for you. Some people find it helpful to discuss a book with their family, as doing so can help put into words experiences they have found difficult to discuss. A few self-help books are given in Chapter 3. It is not possible to give any indication in this section whether a book alone will be the only help you need, but a good self-help book will outline exactly who will find it helpful. The College of Health produces reading and resource lists on a number of topics, including stress and relaxation, and depression.

The specialist services

Everyone knows what doctors and nurses do. Or do they? Nurses have become increasingly specialized with, for example, Community Psychiatric Nurses and Nurse Therapists. What is the difference between a Psychiatrist and a Psychologist or a Psychotherapist? Health service staff sometimes ask these questions, so it is not surprising that the public are puzzled. Members of several different professions work to help people with mental health problems. This can be quite confusing, especially if you are seeing more than one professional.

In this section, based on interviews, individual members of different professions speak about their training and the kind of work they do. Your GP can usually refer you directly to the professionals in this section. There are other professionals who work in the field of mental health, such as occupational therapists and speech therapists. However, it is not usual for your GP to be able to refer you directly to these therapists and for this reason they are not included here.

Each example of the different professions given represents that individual only. It is how *they* work in *their* locality, given *their* resources and interests and the expertise they have developed. For example, the statement by the clinical psychologist about her work in primary care cannot be taken to be true of ALL psychologists in primary care. It is only a guide.

The services of the people mentioned here are all free under the NHS, Social Services or Education Authority, although voluntary organizations sometimes expect a donation. Therapy is available privately in some places, but this subject is not specifically covered here. None of the staff in this section wears a uniform or name badge.

THE MENTAL HEALTH PROFESSIONALS

The relationship between psychology and psychiatry

One of the most common questions asked of clinical psychologists is, 'What's the difference between a psychiatrist and a clinical psychologist?' This is always difficult to explain. Basically, a psychiatrist is a qualified medical doctor who has later specialized in the treatment of mental illness. Clinical psychologists first have to take a degree in psychology, the science of behaviour, rather than medicine. Then they have to do postgraduate studies in applying psychology to the assessment and treatment of psychological difficulties. They see and treat psychological problems more as habits people grow into or develop, than as illnesses which afflict them from outside. But like all the professionals mentioned in this chapter, psychologists and psychiatrists are individuals with their own strengths and interests.

Human beings have been interested in what makes them tick since the beginning of time, but psychology as an experimental science goes back to the end of the last century when the first European experimental psychology laboratories were set up. Clinical psychology is an even more recent development, and is expanding all the time. There have been clinical psychologists in this country since the National Health Service was created in 1948. For many years they worked exclusively alongside psychiatrists, generally in psychiatric hospitals as a member of a psychiatric team. They worked everywhere from the admission wards, where people stayed for only a few weeks, to the long-stay wards devising plans for the rehabilitation of people who had been in hospital for many years. They worked in psychiatric day hospitals and in outpatient clinics. Much useful research which has helped us understand and treat psychological problems has come out of the close relationship between clinical psychologists and psychiatrists.

In more recent years, clinical psychologists have, in addition, been working with a wider range of NHS staff, outside psychiatric hospitals, and to a much larger extent on their own. There has been increasing recognition that the skills of the clinical psychologist can be applied effectively outside psychiatry as mentioned in the Trethowan report (see *The role of clinical psychologists in the health services.* (1977) HMSO). Consequently, clinical psychologists now take more of their referrals directly from GPs.

CLINICAL PSYCHOLOGIST

"My job is working with adults in primary care. That means all the people I see are referred to me by their GPs. They have a variety of problems, including anxiety, phobias, and checking things repeatedly or going over set routines in their mind so often that it badly interferes with their life. Others want help with depression, sexual difficulties, learning to be assertive and self-confident or changing habits such as smoking, over- or under-eating.

People come to me on their own, or with a friend or relative. Sometimes I see people with the person they are already working with – a social worker or a health visitor. I usually see people in a room near the General Hospital, but occasionally I will see them at home or in their GP's surgery. With some problems, I see people in groups; for example, I run an anxiety management group. Many members of this group are also trying to stop taking tranquillizers. Basically I use a cognitive-behavioural approach, but I also use counselling and hypnosis. However, there are some clinical psychologists who take a much more psychodynamic approach.

Occasionally I use psychological tests. These are usually questionnaires and quizzes which the person fills in. Their answers help me to understand their problems better, and so decide on the best treatment for them. Such treatment may involve other professionals. Testing before and after treatment can help show how effective the treatment has been. When clinical psychologists were first employed in the NHS they spent much of their time giving tests, such as those to assess personality or intelligence. Now testing is usually only a small part.

I only spend about half my time seeing clients. The rest of the time is spent in teaching, administration, research, working with other health professionals on projects, in meetings, or keeping up to date by reading and attending courses or conferences. These are all essential parts of the job.

Like many departments, we have a waiting list of clients to be seen. As the whole reason for working in primary care is to see people early on, the waiting list situation is very unsatisfactory. In the long term, we hope this can be reduced by training and supporting other primary care professionals (such as GPs and health visitors) in using psychological therapies. These professionals are more likely to see people when the problems are still new, and possibly easier to deal with. **"**

[PSYCHIATRIST]

"I am based in a centre for community psychiatry, with a team of mental health specialists, including psychiatric nurses, occupational therapists, social workers, a nursery nurse, and a clinical psychologist. Our Centre, in a residential part of town, is in a large old house which used to operate as a day hospital. I see many people here as outpatients, once every few weeks. Many other patients, particularly those with long-term illness, are seen in their own homes or in outlying clinics by the community psychiatric nurses. Social Services also run drop-in centres where many of our patients can meet other people for mutual or self-help. As a consultant at the Centre a considerable amount of my time is spent supervising, supporting and liaising with other members of staff.

A minority of our patients – just under one third – spend some time as an inpatient in hospital, because of severe acute or long-term mental health problems.

People attend here as day patients between 9am and 5pm on weekdays during the first week or whilst being assessed. This is when we look closely at what their difficulties are, so together we can work out a problem list along with suggested steps to resolve the problems. This is discussed with the person involved and with their family if necessary, and forms the treatment contract for that individual. After this, patients only need to come in for particular therapies, as we work out a specific treatment programme for each individual. So one person might come in for one or two activities a week, and take very little time off work, while someone else might need to come every morning.

A treatment contract or programme may include things for a patient to do at home, individual counselling sessions, specific groups to attend, and medication to take, or any combination of these. The patient keeps a copy of their own treatment contract, so they are clear about what we are working towards together. The groups we run include attention training, communications, problem-solving, social skills and anxiety-management. We hold some groups in the evenings. There are also occupational therapy groups, such as those concerned with skills in managing the home or preparing for going to work. We also have keep fit and sport, and a trip into town. The patients themselves have a say in organizing some of the activities.

People have many fears about going to see a psychiatrist. Some believe that it means they are mad, and I spend a lot of time telling people that they are not mad. People see it as very out of the ordinary and are worried about the stigma. Some fear that I am going to put *them away somewhere. But the majority of people I see do not have an actual mental illness, and do not end up in a mental hospital. And most adults will consult a professional about some sort of mental health problem at some time in their life.*

Usually people are referred by their GPs. Up to a quarter of the people we see have themselves asked their doctor to refer them to a psychiatrist, or a relative has asked.

Sometimes a person is referred so that we can give specialist advice on how the GP can help that person. At a number of health centres in the district we offer a referral consultation service to GPs. If a GP has a patient to refer they will discuss the person with a senior psychiatrist, community psychiatric nurse and social worker. Between them they decide if referral is likely to be helpful, and which professional is best suited to help.

What goes on between the GP, the patient and the relatives is important in deciding if someone is referred. The GP's own personality, attitudes and knowledge must play a part too. GPs are also individuals and so differ in the range of help they themselves can offer. For example, one GP I know can treat people with severe depression which most other GPs would refer on to a psychiatrist.

The majority of people who are referred to me have already been prescribed medication or drugs by their GP. For some people I suggest a different drug or a different dosage, and others I suggest come off medication completely. Some people actually ask me for medication, but often people these days say to me, 'I don't want drugs, Doctor'. It isn't inevitable that someone seeing a psychiatrist will have to take drugs. I suppose I prescribe medication for just over half the people I see. I use ECT (electro-convulsive therapy) for some people who are severely depressed, but much of my therapy isn't strictly 'medical' at all. Instead, I use a lot of counselling and psychotherapy.

As a psychiatrist I have a responsibility to see the people who are definitely mentally ill, such as those with psychotic illnesses, the schizophrenias and severe depression. I also work with people who are chronically disabled through mental disorder. But a lot of the referrals to me are not really to do with mental illness, but are concerned with counselling people who may have social and relationship problems. There is an overlap in this area of work with other agencies, such as Marriage Guidance, youth counselling, sexual counselling and the Church. **99**

⟦°COMMUNITY PSYCHIATRIC NURSE°⟧

"A *fter qualifying as a registered mental nurse (RMN), I worked for several years as a sister in a psychiatric hospital, and then in a psychiatric day hospital. It seemed to me that a lot of people were being admitted unnecessarily to psychiatric hospitals at the time. Coming into hospital itself caused a lot of strain to some people and to their families. I could see that there was a lot more that could be done in the community, and so applied for a job as a CPN. After two years' on-the-job experience I went on a year's postgraduate training course in community psychiatric nursing.*

I work with adults with a wide range of problems, from anxiety to schizophrenia. Usually I see them in their own homes, for about an hour each visit. Some people only need weekly visits for about six weeks. I stay involved with others for a much longer time, usually visiting less often. Assessing people's problems at home is a very important part of the job. People are more at ease at home than at a clinic; other members of the family may be present who can help with the problem, or who want to join in the discussion. We provide counselling and support for relatives also. Visits are quite informal, and we are usually on first name terms. If it isn't possible to see someone at home, I will arrange to see them somewhere else – at the clinic or even at their place of work.

In the health district where I work there are 14 CPNs. All my clients are referred to me by psychiatrists. I write to the GP and the psychiatrist to explain my involvement. Then I write again when I have finished seeing a person, and so discharge them. In other places, CPNs work in health centres and clients are referred by GPs.

My work involves counselling, support, and problem-solving. I also give a lot of practical information, such as how to get a home help, or where a lonely person can go to meet people. I try to work out specific goals for each individual. CPNs also run groups for people with similar problems, such as those trying to give up tranquillizers. We also give injections to people suffering from schizophrenia, but not other general nursing duties such as changing dressings.

A big part of the job is liaising with both voluntary and statutory agencies, for example, I might refer an elderly person on to a local Age Concern group. In some cases, I work closely with a social worker and a psychiatrist, or with GPs, and attend all relevant case conferences. To some extent my work overlaps with that of the social worker.

There are a number of specialties within community psychiatric nursing but they are not all found in every health district. These include working with people with mental handicaps, elderly people,

people who have come through the acute psychiatric service or the psychiatric rehabilitation service, adolescents, drug addicts and alcoholics. Some CPNs do further training in different kinds of therapy, such as behaviour therapy.

My own specialty is assessing the problems of people who have recently attempted suicide. One day a week a doctor colleague and I see anyone in the General Hospital who has been admitted following a suicide attempt. We liaise with the consultant psychiatrist by phone, and arrange whatever follow-up is necessary. Some people are referred on to a psychiatrist or to Social Services. Others I see myself when they have left hospital.

I also do some health education – talking to women's groups, school students and trainee health professionals about stress and mental health. The role of the CPN is likely to change and develop in the next few years, and I would like to see it involve more health education. **99**

⸢NURSE THERAPIST⸥

"*I* started by doing my RMN. That is a three-year course to become a registered mental nurse, doing supervised work in a psychiatric hospital whilst studying. During my RMN training I worked in various areas of psychiatry including outpatients, a day centre, acute psychiatry, and geriatrics. It wasn't all in hospital. I did some in the community, going out with community psychiatric nurses. After qualifying, I spent 18 months working as a staff nurse in a psychiatric hospital. Then I left to do 18 months' further training to become a nurse therapist. The course involved one year of study and very carefully-supervised work, and then a six-month placement working in an outpatient department. Again the work was supervised by an experienced therapist.

People are referred to me by their GP, or by a psychiatrist, psychologist or social worker. I work mainly with adults who suffer from anxiety-related problems, particularly those with phobias and obsessive-compulsive problems, with sexual problems, and with habit disorders, such as tics, hair-pulling, thumb-sucking, nail-biting and stammering. I cannot offer anything to people who are acutely psychotic or severely depressed.

I usually work normal office hours and I am based in an NHS outpatient clinic. My first interview with a new client is for screening, to get a basic idea of the problem, and to decide if I have anything to offer them. Generally the treatment I give is short-term. I usually see my clients once a week for eight weeks, and then again for follow-ups after one month, three months and six months. When I am treating someone with a phobia, I might spend about two hours with that person on each appointment for exposure therapy. That means using a skilful approach to face up to whatever is feared so that the anxiety will lessen. Normally psychiatrists do not have the time to conduct this sort of treatment."

MENTAL HEALTH SOCIAL WORKERS

Most qualified social workers have the same basic general training: a two-year CQSW course (Certificate of Qualification in Social Work). The course is about half practical and half theory. For the practical side you are supervised by experienced social workers in a variety of social work settings. The academic side of the course covers child development, ageing, mental health, psychology and sociology, social policy, counselling and welfare rights. It also includes some law, particularly in relation to mental health and child care. Many social workers go on to do further, more specialized training in skills such as counselling, behaviour therapy, sex therapy, family therapy, or group therapy. Some social workers are approved under the 1983 Mental Health Act. That means they have undergone specialist training in mental health, and can, together with a doctor, legally detain people for psychiatric assessment or treatment, in extreme circumstances. The jobs of two mental health social workers working in completely different settings are described next.

⸢°SOCIAL WORKER°⸣

[in a Social Services mental health team]

"We *usually see people in their own homes. People can get in contact with us in a number of ways: they either refer themselves or are referred by someone like a GP or a psychiatrist. Or people can just walk in to the duty room of the local Social Services.*

Many people only see a social worker once: they are then redirected if their help is best obtained from another source, or are given the advice they want then and there. Social workers know a lot about what sort of help is available locally, including self-help groups, voluntary organizations and counselling services. A social worker may not know the answer to your query immediately, but they will usually be able to find out. They may give longer-term counselling.

Where I work, social workers are divided into different specialist teams, for the elderly, mental health, children and families, and handicapped people. We see individuals, couples or families, depending on the need. We also do some work with groups. We may see people weekly or fortnightly, but more often during a crisis.

We have a lot of contact with other professionals such as community psychiatric nurses and psychiatrists, and with voluntary organizations such as MIND. Some social workers are attached all or some of the time to other teams or units where they work alongside other professionals, such as doctors and nurses. For example, one of my colleagues is attached to a sexual dysfunction clinic.

Confidentiality is very important in my work: I will always ask a client's permission if I want to approach anyone else about them, even their doctor. The only exceptions are in extreme circumstances, such as if someone is very ill and their life or health or that of their family is in danger, or they need urgent admission to hospital. Files on clients can usually only be seen by the social worker(s) immediately involved. Access to files is under review, and clients will be able to read their own records in future, providing this does not break confidentiality for anyone else involved.

Some of my clients have very long-standing mental health problems, such as one person who has been in a mental hospital for 20 years and needs help to get back in the community. I have helped him to find somewhere to live, and advised him on his welfare rights. Some of my clients have been admitted to a psychiatric ward or hospital. Often they need practical help, as well as guidance and counselling to readjust.

You can't completely separate mental health from other areas of people's lives. In some ways all social workers are involved in mental health work, not just those in the mental health team. We have resources to help people with problems in looking after their children, problems with an elderly relative, and with people who are physically or mentally handicapped. If a person is under stress because of living with any of these difficulties, or because of bad housing and money problems, they may not need a mental health social worker, but some practical help instead. Improving a person's living conditions can improve their mental health.

In the past, help for people with mental health problems has usually been attached to hospitals. There will always be a need for doctors and nurses, but also many people can be helped by non-medical resources. I see an increase in this sort of facility in the future, particularly at a local level. **99**

[in a community mental health centre]

"People often misunderstand the job of a social worker in mental health. I'm not just 'The person from Welfare come to sort out the money'. Nor am I some sort of police officer whose job is to control people's behaviour. Social work involves a lot of therapy. I studied English and psychology before training to be a social worker, but people come into social work from all sorts of different backgrounds.

After further training in Gestalt therapy, I began work in a residential unit for people recovering from mental illness. Now I work in a community mental health centre, as well as joining in the work of the mental health team. Both of these are part of the local Social Services Department.

The Community Mental Health Centre is in a large town house, where we run a wide range of group therapies for people who come in on a daily basis, as well as for the ten people who live here. The groups include social skills training, assertiveness training, art therapy, tension release and overcoming phobias.

The non-residents either refer themselves to us, or are referred by a social worker or doctor. For many of our clients, we offer an alternative to the psychiatric services. Our clients have a wide range of problems, ranging from severe mental illness and feeling suicidal to wanting to come off tranquillizers.

Clients can only live here for a relatively short time, say six months. They are either here during a current crisis in their lives – a marriage breakup, very difficult family relationships, delayed adolescence – or are needing some form of rehabilitation because of longer-term problems. A panel made up of people from all the mental health professions decides who can be offered a place here. At the beginning of their stay, the resident and their own social worker from the Community Mental Health Centre discuss what they will do with their time here. This is written down as a contract. The contract includes which groups they will join in, and when they will see their key worker for individual counselling. All the people who live here see a psychiatrist as well.**"

63

⟦°MIND WORKER°⟧

❝*I*trained as a social worker, but now work full time for a local branch of MIND, the National Association for Mental Health. We are an independent voluntary organization, and each local branch provides slightly different services, depending on local needs and local resources.

The main things we offer are befriending, counselling, group therapies, help with welfare matters, and general support for people with problems and for their families. Some people use us to help put pressure on others, such as the statutory social services or housing department. We have some paid workers and many volunteers, as well as the members themselves – people become members on payment of a small fee. We sometimes have social workers who work with us under supervision as part of their training. MIND workers come from a wide range of backgrounds and experiences. For example, we have a qualified art therapist working for us, as well as people with no formal mental health qualifications, but with the right experience. We organize training for our workers and volunteers.

Our Management Committee includes a community psychiatric nurse, a psychologist, and a psychiatrist. We have a small voice in how some of the statutory mental health services are organized through our representatives on the Community Health Council (CHC) and some planning teams. My office is in a MIND day centre but I work all over the county.

Most of our users are self-referred, but some people are referred via the health or social services, or by their employers. People who use MIND have a wide range of difficulties. Many are suffering a life trauma, such as job loss, bereavement, the breakup of a relationship, or major illness. They might be at risk of mental illness and recognize that they need to talk to someone. Many of our members are lonely, and MIND can help them make friends.

All our work is confidential. We will ask a person if they want us to contact their GP or social worker, if it will help them. We do not contact others without permission.

Some of our work is in helping people deal with the authorities, particularly the DHSS. We always try to encourage people to do things for themselves, and maybe rehearse with them how they will go about approaching the DHSS, the GP or whoever. In some cases we might make the appointment for the client to see someone in the statutory authority, such as in the Housing Department, and help make it clear what they are going for, or if a person asks us to, we will approach the statutory authority directly. There is a need for this role of advocate, as often we find our clients feel intimidated by people in authority. For example, one woman who wanted to come off tranquillizers found it difficult to get her view across to her doctor, so we contacted him on her behalf.

We have several day centres throughout the county. One is open every day of the year, while others are only open one or two days a week. We have many evening activities. Some of our day centres are especially for elderly, mentally infirm people. Members can make themselves a drink or a meal, or buy a cheap meal from us. There is a lot of participation by members in running the centre.

There are lots of groups run at our day centres. These include problem-centred groups to help with phobias, eating disorders, social skills, pre-menstrual tension, the menopause and agoraphobia. Other groups are more concerned with life skills such as budgeting, cooking, adult literacy (help with filling in forms), or discussions. Members of the agoraphobics group organize the volunteers to give them transport. **99**

⸢°GENERAL PRACTITIONER°⸥

**"*A* **large part of my work as a GP is in helping people with psychological problems for which there are no pills or instant cures. One study asked GPs to estimate how many of the patients they saw had psychological problems. Their estimates varied enormously. Some doctors are very good at recognizing psychological problems, and perhaps attract more patients with such difficulties as they are known to be sympathetic.

There are many advantages in going to see your own doctor first. Some GPs have a special interest or training in helping people with particular problems. The GP usually already knows the person and the family and, of course, they will know their medical history. They also know what resources there are locally, both within the Health Centre, such as a CPN or a marriage guidance counsellor, and specialists outside.

One disadvantage of talking to a GP is lack of time. Both might be very aware of the long queue of people outside the door. In these circumstances I myself might ask the patient to come back later when we can have more time, say at the end of surgery for about half an hour.

Many people just hint that they have a problem, and find it difficult to say directly what the problem is. They might first complain of headaches or insomnia, but then later say there is something else that is worrying them more. Some women start with 'This contraceptive pill isn't suiting me', but further talk reveals problems in a relationship that is making them weepy or unhappy. Perhaps they weren't fully aware of this themselves until they had time to talk.

At every surgery, at least one patient will come into my room, start talking, and burst into tears. A common complaint is feeling tired all the time, and constantly tense. Many mothers of young babies come to see me, complaining of feeling worn out, exhausted or disillusioned. Often it seems that they are trying to do the impossible. They feel under pressure to be the perfect mum. Together we try to sort out what is realistic and help them decide their priorities. As a mother myself, I can say with some authority that it is alright to be imperfect.

Many people who come to me are very lonely, and I try to suggest somewhere suitable for them to go to meet people. Depending on the person, this might be a MIND day centre, or a mothers' and toddlers' group. I have even put several of my patients with similar difficulties in touch with each other, with their agreement, and they have formed a thriving self-help group.

I try to explore with people exactly what the problem is, when it started, and how things used to be. Helping people with psychological problems is a collaborative venture. It doesn't help very much if you just tell people what to do. And there isn't always a clear-cut solution. I like to see them with their husband or wife for a discussion.

I do prescribe tranquillizers or anti-depressants as a short-term measure for some people, say for a week during a very difficult time. I find it can help people to relax enough to begin to get their worries into perspective, and to begin tackling them.

I refer a lot of people to clinical psychologists locally who use a behavioural approach, and this gets results. Teaching people alternative methods of coping with anxiety does seem to have enormous potential. I like it, and the patients like it. When I discuss referral to a clinical psychologist with a patient, I explain that they are not going for a miracle 'cure', but that the psychologist teaches you to sort this out and control it yourself. **99**

Recommended reading

King, S., Pendleton, D. and Tate, P. (1985). *Making the Most of Your Doctor. A family guide to dealing with your GP.* London: Methuen.

⸢ALCOHOL COUNSELLOR⸣

"Alcohol is Britain's biggest drug problem and is the cause of many medical, social and personal problems. About one fifth of our admissions to general hospitals have something to do with the misuse of alcohol. And alcohol plays a significant part in divorce, time off work, road accidents, violence and other crimes. But you don't have to call yourself an alcoholic to be concerned about your drinking.

There are many sources of help for people with drink problems. Some get help from a GP or psychiatrist. Others get help from a specialist NHS alcohol team in the community or in an inpatient unit. Yet others are 'dried out' in a general hospital. There are many well-established voluntary organizations in this area and a national network of alcohol advisory services.

Often the first enquiry is made by the family, spouse or friend, or people refer themselves. They can just phone to make an hour's appointment to talk to a counsellor, usually within the same week. They don't have to tell their GP – some people don't want to have anything about problem drinking on their medical record. However, over 60 per cent of referrals are from doctors. Probation officers also refer some people to us.

About 80 per cent of people with drink problems are in work. So the image of the heavy drinker as a down-and-out is misleading. We get slightly more men than women, but this probably represents a difference between employed and unemployed people, and not really a difference between the sexes. Ten years ago most of our clients were in their 40s while now they are mostly in their 30s.

Our service is run independently and is a registered charity, but we receive a grant from the local District Health Authority. We see anyone whose drinking causes a problem and also those close to them. We recognize both that problems can cause drinking and drinking can cause problems, and we try to offer help for both.

I trained as a clinical psychologist before specializing in this field. Most of the team of counsellors are unpaid. They have all had relevant training and work experience. We have links with other local professionals, such as community psychiatric nurses and probation officers. We offer individual counselling and group therapy, and give talks to anyone who is interested. We are expanding our service to offer help with other sorts of drugs such as tranquillizers or illegal drugs.

The first session with a new client is to assess their drinking, and the effect which it is having on their life. Often there are many other problems as well as the drinking, such as depression, but these problems may improve of their own accord after, say, three weeks off alcohol. At first clients come for weekly appointments for about six weeks, then fortnightly and then once a month. People can stay in touch with us for as long as they like. Some continue then just as members of the group, or come for counselling three or four times a year.

We aim to tailor the treatment programme to suit each individual. For some this means working on controlled drinking, but most people have tried this unsuccessfully before seeing us. For others it is more realistic to aim for complete abstinence – no alcohol at all. One person might need to look into their personality and resentments. Another might need to reconsider their lifestyle and friends. And yet another might need to set goals. When a client has got drinking under control, we often need to look at the other problems related to drink. So someone who drank to help them face social situations might need help with social skills or assertion training. Or we might need to help with depression, loneliness, low confidence or relationship problems. If these aren't tackled, the person is more likely to go back to drinking.

You should be able to find out about services by looking up 'Alcohol' in the phone book. Or ring the Citizen's Advice Bureau, the Samaritans, or the Health Education Department of your local District Health Authority.

There are many health education booklets on sensible drinking, and on helping to prevent problem drinking. I use some of these when I give talks to young people. In my talks, I emphasize that alcohol is a drug, so treat it sensibly and you might then have something that you can enjoy for the rest of your life. If not, you might get hooked and need to give it up for life. **99**

Recommended reading

Heather, N. and Robertson, I. (1986). *Let's Drink To Your Health. A self-help guide to sensible drinking.* Leicester: The British Psychological Society.

MARRIAGE GUIDANCE COUNSELLOR

"*P*eople from the ages of 16 upwards come to the MGC for help with all sorts of relationship difficulties. They can come on their own, or with their partner or another person who is important to them. They don't have to be married or heterosexual. They may come because they are thinking of splitting up and sometimes one person comes after the breakup of a relationship. Counsellors are trained basically using a psychodynamic model, but use a variety of methods, as appropriate. Some have further training to help people with sexual difficulties, and confidentiality is important.

I was always the sort of person whose friends came to talk about their problems, so I thought it would be a good idea to get properly trained and I found out about the thorough selection and training which Marriage Guidance counsellors receive. Our counsellors come from all walks of life. Most of them are volunteers, although the MGC does employ some paid staff.

Our service is free. Clients are asked to make a voluntary contribution, but there is no obligation to do so. About half our clients refer themselves directly, and half are recommended to come by a professional worker or by the Citizen's Advice Bureau. We have a waiting list for counselling, but we do see people for an early first appointment within a week of them contacting us. This is to get an idea of the problem, to give an idea of what counselling involves, and to make sure we are the right service for them. We meet clients in our offices, or in their local health centre, surgery or CAB. If the person is severely disabled we may see them at home. Our interviews take one hour. On average we see people eight to ten times, but our involvement can range from only one session to weekly meetings for 18 months.

We do not aim to give advice. Instead we work with the client(s) to try and understand what is unsatisfactory and why. We try to help them achieve insights into difficult relationships, both current and past. We help clients to accept what they can't change, and make goals to move towards the changes they want and can make. Clients need to do some work between our sessions. This could be an exercise in listening to their partner, or it might be practising a different way of handling a common situation in the home.

The MGC also does a lot of education work. We run a wide range of courses for parents, school students and staff, professional and voluntary workers."

⟨:STUDENT COUNSELLOR:⟩

"I *work as a counsellor in a college of further education. My job is to provide support, acceptance and non-judgmental listening to people for their concerns. People who come to me often have very low self-esteem. I hope I can help them to accept themselves. I do not see this as 'treatment'. It may be all the person needs, or in a few cases it may be a good first step to being referred on to a more specialized helper. I also help students with welfare issues, such as finance and housing. Most colleges have someone to help with welfare problems; but not all have counsellors as such.*

After leaving school I took a degree in social science, and then I worked for several years in educational research. My counselling training for this job was a one-year postgraduate university course. Many of my fellow students had been youth workers or further education lecturers. The course involved both practical and academic work.

Students in this college are aged 16 and above, with an increasing number of mature students. Mostly I see people individually. However, I also run a group for students who have exam anxiety. Some people come of their own accord. Others come because they are recommended by a friend, a lecturer or a youth worker. Or I may just see a member of staff to see if I can assist the student through them, though this would never occur without the student's permission.

People see me for as many 50-minute sessions as necessary, ranging from a single meeting to once a week for several terms. People come to me with a wide range of problems, often to do with relationships. Problems because of sex, such as pregnancy, sexual abuse and incest, also come up. The older students may want to talk about how to cope with the breakup of a marriage. **"**

QUALIFICATIONS

This section gives the most common qualifications you will come across among mental health professionals, and explains what is meant by the letters after people's names. But first a word about general academic qualifications.

General academic qualifications

BA BSc

MA MSc
MPhil

A first degree of Bachelor of Arts or Bachelor of Science usually requires three or four years' full-time study at an institution of higher education, such as a university or polytechnic. Higher degrees include Master of Arts, Master of Science and Master of Philosophy, which take an additional one or two years on top of the first degree. (At Oxford, Cambridge and Scottish universities the MA is a first degree.) A doctorate is a higher degree awarded for research, and is explained next. All these degrees are awarded for a wide range of subjects.

A word about the title 'Doctor'

PhD
DPhil

Not everyone you meet in the NHS called 'Doctor' has a medical training. This can be confusing. The fact is that the title doctor is assumed by those with a first degree in medicine – the medical 'doctors' – and also by those who have gained the higher academic degree Doctor of Philosophy which can be awarded in any subject. The confusion might arise say with a clinical psychologist holding a PhD, who has thereby earned the right to the title but is trained in psychology and not in medicine, and a psychiatrist without a PhD but with a first degree in medicine, who would be given the courtesy title 'Doctor' as a matter of historical precedent.

MEDICAL STAFF

MB,BS

The basic five-year medical school training usually results in the qualification MB,BS. MB stands for Medicinae Baccalaureus; the English Bachelor of

BM BChir BCh MD DM	Medicine (BM) means the same. BS stands for Bachelor of Surgery; the Latin abbreviation BChir or BCh is sometimes preferred. Medical staff then need to work for a further year as a house officer in hospital before becoming a fully-registered medical practitioner. The degree of doctor of medicine (MD or DM) is a higher qualification gained by research, and is not very common.
     MRCPsych FRCPsych	To qualify in psychiatry requires at least another five years' on-the-job training and study after registration as a medical practitioner. Junior doctors go through the usual medical grades of senior house officer, registrar and senior registrar, before becoming a consultant. They can take exams to become first a Member of the Royal College of Psychiatrists (MRCPsych), and then the higher qualification of Fellow of the Royal College of Psychiatrists (FRCPsych).
    MRCGP FRCGP	All new GPs now do three years' post-qualification training on a vocational training scheme, working as a doctor in a number of different settings. Many of them sit the examination to become a Member of the Royal College of General Practitioners (MRCGP), or the advanced qualification of Fellow of the Royal College of General Practitioners (FRCGP).

NURSING STAFF

 RMN	The basic qualification for nurses who work in the field of mental health is that of registered mental nurse (RMN), which takes three years of supervised nursing and study. Many community psychiatric nurses complete a further one-year training. To become a nurse therapist takes 18 months' further training for people with an RMN.
 SEN	The most common other nursing qualifications are those of state enrolled nurse (SEN) which takes

SRN RGN HVCert	two years, and state registered nurse (SRN) or registered general nurse (RGN) which is the three-year, basic, general nursing qualification. Health visitors obtain the certificate in health visiting (HVCert) after qualifying as an SRN.

SOCIAL WORK

CQSW CSS	Most social workers now have a Certificate of Qualification in Social Work (CQSW), normally obtained after a two-year, full-time course at an institution of higher education. Others have the Certificate in Social Service (CSS), which requires part-time study while working.

CLINICAL PSYCHOLOGY

  MSc DipClinPsych	The basic qualifications are a first degree in psychology and postgraduate training leading to either a Master of Science degree (two years, full-time, based at a university or polytechnic) or a Diploma in Clinical Psychology (three years, full-time training organized in the NHS). Both include some time on academic work and research, and the rest in supervised clinical work in the NHS.
 PhD	Some clinical psychologists have higher academic qualifications such as a doctorate (PhD) or a higher degree in another branch of psychology.
    ABPsS FBPsS	The British Psychological Society awards honorary titles (without taking an examination) to psychologists who are considered to be established in the profession: Associate of The British Psychological Society (or ABPsS) and a higher distinction to a few eminent psychologists, Fellow of The British Psychological Society (or FBPsS).

6. Spotlight On Professional Psychologists

So far this book has looked at issues to do directly with therapy and therapists. This chapter now takes a closer look at psychology itself, and mentions some of the professions within psychology. Finally, it answers some of the questions you might have about clinical psychology.

Psychology is like a tree with many branches. Clinical psychology is one main branch, but there are other main branches such as educational psychology, occupational psychology and prison psychology to mention but a few. Each branch also has offshoots, or particular specialist areas. So, for example, there are clinical psychologists who specialize in working with mentally-handicapped people or elderly people. And those specialists might specialize even further.

WHAT IS A PROFESSIONAL?

What is your image of a professional? Someone who is properly qualified and whom you can trust? Someone who dresses smartly and conventionally, and who carries a briefcase? A member of a respected group with standards of work and behaviour to maintain? Someone whose professional organization works to protect clients from unqualified and incompetent people posing as professionals? Or someone who belongs to an elaborate protection racket, working in the interests of the professionals themselves and their own jobs? A professional is someone who is properly qualified and who observes agreed professional standards which can be enforced by a professional body or organization.

REGISTRATION AND CHARTERING

At the moment anyone can call him or herself a psychologist. However, there is a move afoot to change this; or, rather, to protect the term 'Chartered Psychologist'.

The British Psychological Society, the professional organization for psychologists in Great Britain, has applied to the Privy Council for a Charter in order to set up a *Register of Chartered Psychologists,* which would provide the public with a professional guarantee of qualifications.

To be eligible to be entered on the *Register,* psychologists would have to spend at least six years in both studying and practising psychology. A first degree alone would not be sufficient to qualify for the title Chartered Psychologist.

The *Register* would cover all branches of psychology: clinical, educational and occupational, as well as many others. So, if you wanted to make sure of a particular clinical psychologist's qualifications, you would also need to check whether he or she is a member of the Division of Clinical Psychology of the Society; only clinical psychologists are entitled to join this Division, though not all who are entitled do so.

Moreover, in the early days of the *Register,* it would not be compulsory for psychologists to register. This may seem an unsatisfactory state of affairs, but it reflects the relative infancy of the profession.

Similarly, as yet there is no register of counsellors or psychotherapists as such, although many will be members of other registered professions. However, there are a number of professional organizations to which they can belong. These organizations require certain minimum qualifications as well as having their own codes of conduct or rules for members. The professional organizations include:

The British Association for Behavioural Psychotherapy

The British Association for Counselling

The British Society of Experimental and Clinical Hypnosis

The Family Therapy Association

The Psychology and Psychotherapy Association.

Clinical psychologists and other professionals who work in the National Health Service have to possess full professional qualifications as a condition of employment. This is also true of other psychologists employed in the public sector, such as in the education service, social services or prisons. So, even without a *Register* you can be sure that psychologists employed in the public sector are properly trained.

A word about private practice

It is not so easy to be sure of a psychologist's qualifications in the private sector, or for people who are self-employed, as anyone can call themselves a psychologist regardless of qualifications. Here the *Register* would provide a useful guarantee.

MORE ABOUT CLINICAL PSYCHOLOGY

Most clinical psychologists in the UK work in the NHS, but a few are employed in the social services, and others work privately.

? How many clinical psychologists are there?

Clinical psychology is a relatively small profession in Britain. In 1985 there were about 1,500 full time clinical psychologists working in the National Health Service in England. There were also 243 posts still unfilled. Clinical psychologists are not evenly distributed around the country. In some health districts there are large departments which can offer a comprehensive service. In some places there are only a few, and some health districts do not employ any clinical psychologists. In these areas, a person would be referred to one of the other mental health professionals.

Clinical psychologists work with a number of different client groups, and about a quarter work in more than one area. Their main areas of work, in order of the number of psychologists involved, are in adult psychiatric services, mental handicap services, and in child and family guidance. They also work with the elderly, and in general hospitals. Some see people who are referred directly by their GPs. Finally, they work with people involved with the law, and with alcohol or drugs. Clinical psychologists working in all these areas are also involved in teaching other health professionals.

❓ How are clinical psychologists trained?

To begin training in clinical psychology you usually need a first degree in psychology. You can then either take a two- or three-year postgraduate course at a university or polytechnic or join a three-year NHS in-service training course and sit the Society's Diploma in Clinical Psychology examination. Clinical training involves academic work, clinically-relevant research, and practical experience in a work setting under the close supervision of a qualified and experienced psychologist. These practical placements include working with adults in a mental health setting, with children, and with mentally-handicapped people. It might also be possible to do more specialized placements, such as in a general hospital, in physical or psychiatric rehabilitation, or attached to a general practice.

❓ Who works in a District Psychology Service?

Qualified clinical psychologists are sometimes referred to by their grade or seniority. From the least to the most senior, clinical psychologists are called:

☐ Basic Grade Clinical Psychologist

☐ Senior Clinical Psychologist

☐ Principal Clinical Psychologist

☐ Top Grade Clinical Psychologist

☐ Top Grade Clinical Psychologist with extra responsibility.

The person in charge of clinical psychology services for a health district is usually called a District Psychologist.

A psychological technician is another person you might find in a department of clinical psychology. These are often people who are gaining experience after taking a first degree in psychology, and before going on to train in clinical psychology. Nurse therapists are sometimes based in psychology departments, and you might come across people doing research. Everyone in the psychology department should maintain confidentiality about clients, as discussed later in more detail.

? *Will I always see the same psychologist?*

YES, almost always. This 'continuity of care' is standard among psychologists, unlike many other professions where you might see a different person at each appointment. But psychological treatment usually involves building a relationship between you and your therapist, so continuity is vital. However there are inevitable exceptions; your psychologist may be away for a long period, or might leave the district. But whenever possible he or she would discuss this with you beforehand.

? *Will what I say be kept confidential?*

The answer to this is YES, within the limits required by law. Files are kept safely, usually under lock and key, in the psychology department. Technically these files belong to the Health Authority on behalf of the Secretary of State for Social Services. Do say if there is any information you do not want to be recorded. The psychologist may need to discuss information related to your therapy with other professionals who are involved with you. Only in exceptional circumstances might the rules of confidentiality be broken in order to prevent serious harm to yourself or someone else, or in the event of serious crime.

All health authorities and their employees are legally bound by 'The Code on Confidentiality of Personal Health Information' and 'The Data Protection Act'. Both of these are legal documents and can be bought from HMSO booksellers. The first of these was issued under the National Health Service Act. It makes it clear that health authorities hold personal information *only* for the purposes of health care, and the client or patient has a *right* to have such information kept confidential and disclosed only for health care. This statutory code is consistent with existing professional codes of ethics, such as the BPS's *Code of Conduct.*

Under the 1984 Data Protection Act, people have a right to know what information is held about them on computers, and to be supplied with a copy of it. If necessary they can correct errors. However the Home Secretary can make exceptions in the case of information about physical and mental health. A group of professionals (the Interprofessional Working Group on Access to Personal Health Information), concerned with people's access to computerised health information under the Data Protection Act, made several recommendations to the DHSS. Their view is that in principle it is good that people should have access to information about them. However, they say that in some cases records could harm a client or someone else. Records can include information about another person (a third party) which should not be passed on to the client, and health professionals must bear this in mind in giving people access to their computerised files. If a person wants to find out more about their files than the professional they see thinks fit, the group recommended that an independent professional sees the data on the client's behalf. If the client is still unhappy, the group recommends going to court to get access to the information. At the time of writing, very little client information is held on computers by clinical psychologists.

The BPS has published *Guidelines for the Professional Practice of Clinical Psychology* and *A Code of Conduct for Psychologists*. They apply to all clinical psychologists who belong to the Society, and they maintain the rules of confidentiality. A psychologist would need a client's consent to discuss their case with anyone else, including relatives. Other professional organizations to which clinical psychologists may belong will also have their own code of conduct for their members.

? *Will they do anything to me without my consent?*

The answer here is almost always NO. Their code of conduct requires them to obtain your consent. Under the law, the only circumstances in which a person can be treated without their consent is if they are detained under the Mental Health Act (1983). This applies to a very tiny percentage of the people seen by clinical psychologists, and would not be the case for the people whose therapies are discussed in this book.

? *Will they use me for teaching or research?*

When any health professional teaches others, they usually illustrate what they are talking about with real-life accounts. However, this is normally done in such a way that the person involved remains anonymous. This is also usually true when writing about people in research case studies and books like this. The original clients cannot be identified. Any research in the NHS has to be agreed by an ethical committee. If this is so, and the person involved cannot be identified or caused damage or distress, then information about them can be used without their permission. However, it is more usual to ask for a person's informed consent. Sometimes your therapist might ask if a colleague or trainee may sit in on your sessions as this is an excellent way of learning about how other people work. You should be under no obligation to agree.

? *What if I'm not happy with my psychologist?*

You can expect certain standards of behaviour from a psychologist, as a professional. But if you are not happy with the therapy or with some aspect of your psychologist's behaviour, it is preferable first to discuss your feelings with the individual concerned. You may be able to clear up disagreements or misunderstandings this way. Ask someone to come with you if you don't feel you can go alone, or phone them, or write to them. If you want a second opinion about what sort of therapy is suited to you, ask your own psychologist if they can arrange it, or contact the District Psychologist to discuss this. Try to let your own psychologist know that this is what you want.

If you then want to make a complaint about your clinical psychologist there are several courses open to you. First, you could contact the District Psychologist. Or you could write directly to the Unit General Manager of the unit for which the psychologist works. If you do not know which management unit this is, contact your local Community Health Council (CHC) to find out. A psychologist who is found to be at fault by the District Health Authority will be subject to a disciplinary procedure. CHCs are the consumer's watchdog for the NHS.

If you feel there has been serious misconduct on the part of the psychologist, you could contact The British Psychological Society, but they can only take action if the psychologist concerned is a member.

? *What is my side of the relationship?*

We've already discussed some of the psychologist's obligations towards you, and how you can complain if a psychologist behaves unprofessionally. But to be successful, the relationship with a psychologist is two-way. Your part is to be honest, and to keep your appointments. If you can't attend an appointment, try to let the psychologist know as soon as possible so another time can be arranged and your old appointment offered to someone else.

AUTHOR'S POSTSCRIPT

If you are looking for help with a psychological problem, I hope this book has assisted in your search. It set out to help you find your way through the maze of services. In particular, I hope that you:

- [ ] don't feel alone with or frightened by your problem
- [ ] have a clearer idea of what your want from a helper, and feel you can work *with* your helper
- [ ] find the most suitable help.

GOOD LUCK.

Further reading

Eysenck, H.J. (1977). *You and Your Neurosis.* London: Temple Smith. [A thorough book about the behavioural approach to neuroses, written for the layperson.]

Gibbs, A. (1986). *Understanding Mental Health.* London: Consumers Association and Hodder & Stoughton. [This book briefly covers a very wide range of mental health topics. It looks at the causes and types of mental illness and other emotional problems, treatments, getting help, compulsory hospital care, and living with mental illness for both the sufferer and friend or relative.]

Melville, J. (1980). *First Aid in Mental Health.* London: Allen & Unwin. [Cheap paperback. A guide to the nature and problems of mental illness and to who can help and the treatments. Looks in detail at schizophrenia, anxiety and stress, depression, anorexia, and the elderly mentally infirm. Has a section on patients' rights and useful addresses.]

Open University. (1980). *The Good Health Guide.* London: Harper & Row. [Comprehensive and attractive book which helps you look at your own health, both physical and mental, and suggests how to make changes to improve your health.]

MIND Factsheet 1. *Mental Illness.* London: Mind Publications.

Books by post

The following places stock books on mental health, relationships, sexuality or therapy. Send a s.a.e. for their booklists.

MIND National Association for Mental Health
Publications Mail Order Service
4th Floor, 24–32 Stephenson Way
LONDON
NW1 2HD
Tel: 01 387 9126

The Book Department
National Marriage Guidance Council
Little Church Street
Rugby
Warwickshire
CV21 3AP
Tel: 0788 73241

The Book Centre
The Family Planning Association
27–35 Mortimer Street
LONDON
W1N 7RJ
Tel: 01 636 7866

INDEX